Praise for

Stop Talking, Start Communicating

"Geoffrey Tumlin delivers practical solutions for astutely and appropriately balancing our increasing communication loads with a combination of digital tools and direct human contact. *Stop Talking, Start Communicating* is essential reading for executives, aspiring managers, and anyone else who wants smart, workable strategies for better communication in the digital age."

—Marshall N. Carter, former chairman and CEO
of State Street Bank and Trust Company

"Finally! An instruction manual for our crazy digital world! Geoffrey Tumlin nails the problem—an avalanche of fast and frivolous communication is creating major relationship strains—and he provides page after glorious page of solutions. I haven't read a book this important in years."

—Chris Miller, founding partner of the Praevius Group

"The digital age has forever changed the nature of everyday communication. This new terrain requires a reliable and up-to-date road map with practical solutions to our communication problems. And that's exactly what Geoffrey Tumlin gives us in *Stop Talking, Start Communicating*. This is a groundbreaking, must-read book for everyone, which provides the tools for building better relationships in our new and challenging communication environment."

—Mark L. Knapp, emeritus professor of communication
at the University of Texas at Austin and former president
of the National Communication Association
and the International Communication Association

"*Stop Talking, Start Communicating* is business writing at its very best: incredibly insightful, eminently practical, and thoroughly readable. Get your hands on this book; you'll find something useful on every page."

—John Knighten, former vice president
at St. Jude Medical and Boston Scientific

"What a weird combination—a West Point–trained infantry ranger with a communication PhD—but these two backgrounds come together to create an informative, funny, and spot-on book about communication, relationships, and life. You'll start to read it and not be able to put it down. It's filled with great examples and practical advice you'll use an hour from now—at work, at home, everywhere in your life. A modern-day Dale Carnegie!"

—John Daly, Liddell Professor of Communication and
Texas Commerce Bancshares Professor of Management
at the University of Texas at Austin

"Geoffrey is a five-tool consultant: brilliant strategist, inspiring teacher, keen listener, incisive coach, and gifted writer. *Stop Talking, Start Communicating* is like a greatest hits collection of Geoffrey's advice for productive working and meaningful living. Buy this book for everyone you care about."

—Manuel Morin, former managing director of the
Dallas Cowboys and president of Control Ergonomics

"*Stop Talking, Start Communicating* is delightfully well-written and filled with useful antidotes to the communication challenges that bedevil so many of us today. With wit, precision, and a gentle touch, Geoffrey Tumlin adroitly leads readers toward better communication and more meaningful work and home relationships. *Stop Talk-*

ing, Start Communicating is an extremely valuable book written by a very thoughtful communicator."

—Howard T. Prince II, Loyd Hackler Endowed Chair in Ethical Leadership at the University of Texas at Austin and founding dean of the Jepson School of Leadership Studies

"Geoffrey Tumlin knows his stuff. We've got a problem with our communication today and Geoffrey has the solutions. With his characteristic good humor and penetrating pragmatism, Geoffrey loads *Stop Talking, Start Communicating* with tips and strategies to improve our interactions with each other. Geoffrey has written an important, timely, and outstanding book. Read it!"

—Jefferson Howell, former director of the Johnson Space Center and former Marine Forces Pacific Commander

"*Stop Talking, Start Communicating* is filled with no-nonsense advice, actionable communication strategies, and plenty of wit and humor to keep you turning the pages. Geoffrey's straightforward solutions for more productive interactions in the digital age are just what we need to cut through information overload in an increasingly fragmented work environment. Grab a copy of this book and start improving the quality of the time you spend with colleagues today."

—Jason Santamaria, vice president of business transformation at Stanley Black & Decker and author of *The Marine Corps Way*

"Geoffrey Tumlin presents the solutions we need to significantly improve our work and home interactions. *Stop Talking, Start Communicating* is useful reading for everyone seeking a path to better communication."

—James V. Kimsey, founding CEO and chairman emeritus of America Online, Inc.

"*Stop Talking, Start Communicating* is an extraordinary analysis of the impact of the digital revolution on our humanness. But Geoffrey Tumlin goes way beyond analysis and charts the path forward with clear guideposts and convincing directions for improving our vital communication skills. Countless times throughout the book, been-there-done-that moments jumped out at me, along with straightforward instructions for handling those situations more effectively in the future. *Stop Talking, Start Communicating* shows us how to regain the human essence of our communication in a constructive and meaningful way."

—Charles W. McClain Jr., special advisor to the president,
CEO of Texas A&M Galveston, and
former Chief of Public Affairs, U.S. Army

"I hear Geoffrey's wise, patient, and authentic voice on every page of *Stop Talking, Start Communicating*. Geoffrey's clear-headed thinking and timely counsel have made a major positive impact on the life of Grace After Fire. It's great to have so many of his shrewd ideas collected in a book—now you too can benefit from his uniquely insightful and effective advice."

—Kimberly Olson, CEO/president of Grace After Fire

"Effective leaders build credibility and strengthen relationships through dozens of daily interactions. *Stop Talking, Start Communicating* is an essential guidebook to help you get the most out of these important encounters. Geoffrey Tumlin clears a path to the kind of good, consistent communication that fuels outstanding individual and organizational accomplishments."

—Robert Forsten, U.S. Army psychiatrist

"In an age of groundbreaking communication technologies, we need groundbreaking communication skills. Geoffrey Tumlin eloquently explores these vital competencies in *Stop Talking, Start Communicating*, sharing essential knowledge and priceless advice for creating and maintaining thriving connections in the digital age. *Stop Talking, Start Communicating* should be a part of everyone's communication game plan."

—Adeline Cassin, commercial vice president of digital communications at Discovery Networks Latin America

"In *Stop Talking, Start Communicating*, Geoffrey Tumlin perfectly describes and provides remedies for a hyper-connected digital environment where our digital communication capabilities often seem to exceed our interpersonal communication abilities. Insightful, authoritative, and a pleasure to read from cover to cover, *Stop Talking, Start Communicating* is the book you've been waiting for."

—Mark Warren, training coordinator at the Texas Association of Counties

"I saw myself on every page of this book. What a relief to have clarity on communication problems I see everywhere, and what a gift to have so many practical communication tools all in one place! Swiftly, surely, and with much-appreciated humor, *Stop Talking, Start Communicating* helped me reduce communication mistakes and steer clear of conversational trouble. Don't wait to buy this crucial book. It will help you from the very first page."

—Boris G. Robinson, owner and president of T3Multisports and board member of Tri for Success

"*Stop Talking, Start Communicating* is a remarkably insightful book written by a consummately gifted communicator. The pages overflow with keen observations, practical strategies, and great ideas for communication improvement. This is a book I'll refer to constantly!"

—Lynne Liberato, former president of the State Bar of Texas

"Geoffrey Tumlin's practical communication advice is unrivaled. His methods challenge conventional wisdom and drive to the very heart of who we are—and who we hope to be—in business, in friendships, and in our families. *Stop Talking, Start Communicating* is mandatory reading for success in what matters most in life. Highly recommended!"

—Harry Ben Adams IV, vice president of real estate and development at McCombs Enterprises

"What a book! Channeling the warm practicality of Stephen Covey and the engaging wit of Tom Peters, Geoffrey Tumlin's *Stop Talking, Start Communicating* is a must-read for anyone concerned with how we are communicating today. Buy this book and read it from cover to cover!"

—Sherri Baer, vice president at Virginia Cook Realtors

"In *Stop Talking, Start Communicating*, Geoffrey Tumlin distills insights from his diverse experience in the military, in the academy, and in boardrooms into a thoughtful and insightful analysis of effective communication. With ample wit and a sharp eye, Geoffrey provides simple, straightforward solutions to what remains a complex problem in many of our daily lives: in a world where instant and constant communication is easier than ever, why is it so hard to really connect?"

—Stuart Shapiro, commercial real estate developer at United Equities, Inc.

"Geoffrey helped me improve my business, and more important, he helped me improve my life. A gifted communicator with a remarkable ability to connect quickly and meaningfully with people, Geoffrey practices what he preaches. *Stop Talking, Start Communicat-*

ing didn't just come from Geoffrey's brain . . . it came from the way he lives his life."

—Ned Lavelle, owner of Pinthouse Pizza
and multiple Jimmy John's franchises

"Geoffrey's consulting and advice helped All-Pro successfully navigate a critical turning point in our business. Geoffrey takes everything in, listening so closely and absorbing information so completely that when he finally talks, workable solutions quickly emerge in places that had previously been knotted with problems. Thanks, Geoffrey, for writing this book, and thanks for putting so many of your great ideas together in one place."

—Kyle Anderson and Brandon Berryman,
owners of All-Pro Auto Reconditioning

"*Stop Talking, Start Communicating* is a masterpiece of practical advice. Geoffrey Tumlin's insights are clear, compelling, and exactly what we need to improve our communication today. This book should be mandatory reading for anyone interacting with people on a regular basis—in other words, everyone should read it! It's in our department's leadership library, and I highly recommend it for your library as well."

—Robert Isbell, fire chief of Midland, Texas,
and president of the Texas Fire Chiefs Association

"In *Stop Talking, Start Communicating*, Geoffrey Tumlin perfectly balances thought and action to deliver an easy-to-read communication improvement masterpiece that's as street smart as it is book smart. Crammed with sharp insights, strategies, and tools that anyone can use, *Stop Talking, Start Communicating* is an enormously valuable book. I wholeheartedly recommend it!"

—Sean Lux, assistant professor at the Center for
Entrepreneurship at the University of South Florida

"*Stop Talking, Start Communicating* is the perfect book for our time. Geoffrey Tumlin spells out strategies we can immediately use to strike the right balance between our powerful digital devices and the important people they connect us to. With a wealth of practical experience and clear and important insights for interpersonal relationships, Geoffrey shows us how to navigate the chaotic and distracting digital communication environment we face today."

—Kathy Whitmire, former mayor of Houston
and former board member of the
New York Stock Exchange

STOP
TALKING
START
COMMUNICATING

STOP
TALKING
START
COMMUNICATING

COUNTERINTUITIVE SECRETS TO SUCCESS IN BUSINESS AND IN LIFE

GEOFFREY TUMLIN

FOREWORD BY MARTHA MENDOZA

New York Chicago San Francisco Athens London Madrid Mexico City
Milan New Delhi Singapore Sydney Toronto

3 4 5 6 7 8 9 0   DOC/DOC   1 9 8 7 6 5 4

ISBN 978-0-07-181304-4
MHID 0-07-181304-7

e-ISBN 978-0-07-181305-1
e-MHID 0-07-181305-5

Library of Congress Cataloging-in-Publication Data
Tumlin, Geoffrey.
   Stop talking, start communicating : counterintuitive secrets to success in business and in life / by Geoffrey Tumlin.
      pages cm
   Includes bibliographical references and index.
   ISBN 978-0-07-181304-4 (alk. paper) — ISBN 0-07-181304-7 (alk. paper) 1. Business communication. 2. Success in business. 3. Communication. 4. Success. I. Title.
   HF5718.T87 2013
   650.101'4—dc23

                          2013010256

Names of people, identifying information about companies, and minor details in examples have been changed throughout this book to maintain confidentiality. A portion of the author's royalties will be donated to Critical Skills Nonprofit, a 501(c)(3) public charity founded by the author to provide communication and leadership skills training to chronically underserved populations.

McGraw-Hill Education books are available at special quantity discounts to use as premiums and sales promotions or for use in corporate training programs. To contact a representative, please visit the Contact Us pages at www.mhprofessional.com.

This book is printed on acid-free paper.

To Daphne, Evelyn, Cindi, Karen, Welela, and Iris,
Three generations of strong women
And Ron,
For pointing the way

CONTENTS

FOREWORD

I'm constantly communicating, negotiating, and managing conflict, whether it's convincing a colleague to tone down a provocative proposal or getting my five-year-old to button up her itchy sweater. Much of this communication I do without intentional thought, and often—as I look back on it—I can see that my motivations were sometimes skewed.

- ➤ Pitching a project idea at work? My pride is at stake.
- ➤ Bargaining at a Mexico City market? I want to win.
- ➤ Arguing with a colleague? I don't want to back down.
- ➤ Renting a California beach bungalow? I don't want to be a sucker.

Whenever I bought a car or asked for a raise, I was aware I was engaged in a formal, consequential business interaction. It's like the evening chess games my son and I play: I make my move, he makes his, but we're both thinking a few moves ahead.

But for most of my daily communication—in the office, at my kids' school, or at home—my dealings aren't deliberate. I'm not considering what I want, or what others are after. And there can be strange reasons for my moves: Perhaps this person bought me a cup of coffee yesterday, or maybe I feel sorry for him—he seems a little stressed out. Sometimes I'm involved in a self-made competition, so I dig in relentlessly.

I'm a wife, a mother of four kids, a journalist for a major international news organization, a daughter, sister, and friend. I like to run in the forest and snorkel above coral reefs. I sing really loudly in the morning while I make breakfast, and I fall asleep in movie theaters. Each of these apparently simple pleasures has its communication pitfalls. The wife, mother, and journalist ones seem obvious: a steady stream of discussions over where we'll spend Thanksgiving, whether that chemistry homework is complete, and how to frame an investigative project. But what about when a mountain bike class is bombing down my favorite redwood forest running trail? Or when the snorkel gear rentals are suddenly exorbitant? Or if my neighbors don't want to hear me belting out '70s hits before dawn? And what does my husband really think about me falling asleep at the movies, again?

An avid baker, I'm a believer in recipes. I've done Julia Child's 17-page French bread and the King Arthur Flour's five-day sourdough bagels. The resulting goodies, toasted with butter, are all the proof I need that following directions, step-by-step, is worth it.

Yet it's been a revelation to realize there's a recipe for communication.

There came a day when I was mired, truly mired, in a spiraling, escalating issue. I was furious, hurt, and self-righteous. I was also stuck. I sought help from Geoffrey Tumlin, frantically laying out my case.

Geoffrey is a remarkably gifted communicator, an astute listener, and a master at lining up the right conversational tactics to support a larger, more important goal. His easygoing Texas warmth and natural sense of humor blend with a rigorous West Point background and a top-flight academic mind to create a delightful mix of insight, understanding, and accessibility. Geoffrey Tumlin knows how communication works and how good communication can work for you.

Over years of study and practice, Geoffrey has formed a deliberate and straightforward method for strengthening interpersonal communication skills. Now these methods, which he's brought as a consultant to major, international companies, are distilled into simple-to-follow recipes. Easier than bagels!

Geoffrey hadn't written this book yet the day I called him. But he knew the principles. Calmly and thoughtfully, he listened to my outrage. What he suggested was, initially, a little hard to swallow. I was part of the problem. I was responsible for the solution.

But then, step-by-step, we walked through the moves I could make to get what I wanted. And following his guidance, which is now pinned to the wall of my cubicle, I got there. No. *We* got there. In the end, the person I was communicating with and I were both satisfied with the solution.

It meant muting my good comebacks. Sarcasm was out. So was being snide. I needed to be honest, I needed to be clear, and I needed to listen. Then and only then, as Geoffrey so patiently explained, would I be in a position to make the most of the situation.

It worked.

As a journalist, I once had an opportunity, collaborating with three brilliant and dogged colleagues, to gather enough archival, interview, and physical evidence to document a disturbing and powerful war crime. We wrote our news story and handed it to our editors, who were skeptical. Their concern was protecting the credibility of our entire company. Our concern was getting this story out and letting the truth be told. We spent months fighting—not communicating—over this. Finally, after a different editor stepped in to mediate, we found a way to compromise, to get the story out, and to bring about a small resolution for the soldiers who had fired and the civilians who had been fired upon.

The story went on to win a Pulitzer Prize "for revealing, with extensive documentation, the decades-old secret of how American soldiers early in the Korean War killed hundreds of Korean civilians in a massacre at the No Gun Ri Bridge."

While the recognition came for our investigative work, I know, as do my colleagues, that the real success was breaking our internal logjam and moving from fighting about the story to resolving our differences and helping the story see the light of day. What a difference good communication makes.

"The ways that we communicate—and the ways that we don't—shape our relationships, and our relationships shape our lives," says Geoffrey Tumlin in this wise, important book. "The most important people in our lives deserve our very best communication."

I'm working on it.

—Martha Mendoza

INTRODUCTION

I n the 1970s, when I was six years old and you could meet arriving passengers at the airport gate, my dad and I waited at Houston's Intercontinental Airport for my uncle to arrive from North Carolina. When the plane pulled in, I worked my way to the front of the crowd. I could see his big smile yards away, and I ran to meet him.

"You got here fast," I said as I gripped him in my best bear hug.

"Next time I'll come on a spaceship," he replied, "and get here even faster."

My uncle probably wasn't the only person at the airport that day who, if asked to make a prediction about the future, would have guessed that spaceships or jet packs might soon beam us around the globe.

But they would have been wrong. Forty years later, we still get from one place to another pretty much the same way, from the fossil fuels to the uncomfortable seats. Instead of revolutionary ways to transport our bodies around the earth, humans spent the past few decades figuring out how to speed our words and images around the planet. The transportation revolution never arrived. We got a communication revolution instead.[1]

Around the time that I was greeting my uncle at the gate, the world's first generation of computer geeks was busy trying to configure a personal machine that wouldn't break our desks and a phone that didn't need a cord. Advances in computing and telecommunications gathered speed through the 1980s and 1990s. Then, in the mid-1990s, the Internet arrived, kicking off the digital communication revolution in earnest.

Almost two decades later, here we are, inundated with smartphones, laptops, iPads, VOIP, text messaging, Facebook, Twitter, apps, and countless other technologies that allow us to connect quickly, cheaply, and easily across the globe. These advances have been incredibly beneficial, enabling *billions* of people to communicate with each other, share information, and spread ideas.

The communication revolution transformed our lives so thoroughly and so quickly that we're still scrambling to understand the changes that our powerful new tools unleashed. What we do know, though, is that the changes are not uniformly positive.

The digital Promised Land turns out to be infested with a kudzulike thicket of unintended consequences. Just as the "miracle vine"[2] eventually ended up as the "vine that ate the South,"[3] our remarkable digital devices are beginning to overpower, entangle, and suffocate some of our best—and our most human—communication behaviors.

The very tools that enable us to maintain contact with people all over the world also serve, at times, to scatter our limited attention across too many areas. We fiddle with our smartphones during meetings and upset our coworkers. We bungle an interaction with an important colleague because we're distracted by an e-mail. We interrupt a fruitful collaboration to respond to a trivial text message. We use a social media platform to reconnect with an old work acquaintance, only to offend her with an ill-advised attempt at humor or a provocative statement of our political beliefs. We type an e-mail to a client while talking to a coworker on the phone, loading the e-mail with typos while simultaneously mangling the phone conversation.

Today, it is possible to accumulate scores of friends and still feel lonely; be connected to hundreds of people and feel like no one is listening; and spend hours at work, sending and responding to countless messages, but still feel unproductive. The revolution has made it easy to communicate with other people, but the meaningful—or even just effective—connections we desire seem to be more elusive than ever.

What kind of a revolution is this?

Blood in the Tweets

The digital communication revolution changed our lives, but it brought three significant types of collateral damage.[4]

Our Environment Is Increasingly Inhospitable to Productive and Meaningful Communication

The communication revolution created an environment that's paradoxically inhospitable to effective communication. In hindsight, it's easy to see how this happened. Humans love to talk, and we crave connections with others. We were given powerful new tools to do just that, and in no time flat, the rate and volume of our communication exploded. We started *hypercommunicating*.

But a hypercommunicating environment leads to message overload and distracted conversations, which, in turn, cause error-prone interactions.[5] These errors add stress to our lives and inflate existing problems, amplifying hypercommunication's negative cycle of overload-error-problem.

Evidence keeps piling up about the debilitating impact of digital distractions on our concentration, about the toll that multitasking places on our cognition, and about the ways that our addictions to electronic rewards and online diversions distort our priorities.[6] Our concentration fragments, our ability to listen degrades, and our attention scatters.

Many of us have a nagging sense that it's getting harder to communicate well, to prevent our quick-draw tongues from saying harmful things, or to stop our fingers from hammering out impulsive messages. And we're right. Researchers have demonstrated that our willpower is finite and that it becomes depleted as we draw upon it.[7] The mind-numbing, limitless options and the tantalizing temptations of the digital age are burning through our reserves of willpower, degrading our decisions, and making us distracted and unproductive.

Even though I make my living as a communication consultant, I can see the impact in my own life. Two decades ago, the undergraduate version of me could focus and write a complete research paper in one sitting, but today I can't produce a grocery list without stopping to check my e-mail twice. Without any natural military acumen, as a younger man I willed myself through Ranger School, but now I can't manage to will myself to finish a simple paragraph without clicking over to Google News to see what's happening. And even while I'm writing about how distractions harm our closest relationships, I still have difficulty resisting my vibrating cell phone when I'm talking with my wife, and I find it hard to avoid checking for new messages when I'm on a call with a client.

In almost every other area of my life, I am shaking off counterproductive behaviors and becoming a better, more complete person. I've never been more sensible, more grounded, or more mature. So why on earth do I feel like I was more productive 20 years ago, when I was less developed in virtually every way?

The answer: Twenty years ago there weren't so many tempting distractions, or so many seductive ways to yield to an impulse. The digital communication revolution ushered in a world of endless choices and captivating diversions that require an almost heroic level of self-control and focus to counteract.[8] It's hard to imagine an environment less conducive to productive and meaningful communication than our current setup.

Speed and Convenience Have Become Guiding Communication Principles

Humans are an eminently adaptable, shortcut-loving species. Give us a barrier, and we'll find a way around it; show us a leak, and we'll devise a patch. So when the digital revolution led to hypercommunication and message overload, we found a workaround. We downshifted to the quickest, cheapest, and easiest ways to communicate.[9]

Too many e-mails? Reply with one-sentence messages, stop capitalizing (or TURN ON CAPS LOCK), and throw out your grammar book. Phone ringing? Let it go to voice mail and reply with a text message. Too busy to tell your close friends about a promotion? Post the news on Facebook. Have an idea? No need to think it over; just send out a tweet. And who really needs words anyway? LOL.

But embracing quick, cheap, and easy communication as the default way to cope in our hypercommunicating environment has serious downsides. *Quick* communication discourages reflection and thoughtfulness and is notoriously error prone; *cheap* communication provides little or no incentive to get the message right the first time; and *easy* communication has fooled us into thinking that interactions require little or no effort.

Productive and meaningful communication has never been easy. But adopting speed and convenience as guiding principles is degrading our communication and straining our relationships.

Interpersonal Communication Is Marginalized by the Rise of Personal and Mass Communication

Building a productive and meaningful life requires effective *interpersonal* communication. Interpersonal communication takes the other person's perspective into account and can be either one-on-one dialogue or interactions among a small number of people.[10] Interpersonal communication is the foundation of our relational lives—it's how we build our relationships—in a way that *mass* communication (sending tweets, giving presentations, composing Facebook posts, and otherwise broadcasting messages to more people than you can easily count) and *personal* communication (conversations that don't take the other person's perspective into account; monologues and self-expressive chatter) will never be.

Interpersonal communication is the focus of *Stop Talking, Start Communicating* because that's where the action is. I can't lecture my way into a good relationship with my boss or a key client; I build those productive bonds one interpersonal conversation at a time. I can't PowerPoint my way into being a good husband, but meaningful conversations with my wife will eventually build up an interpersonal "body of work"—a goodwill account—that facilitates a strong marriage.

Unfortunately, the digital communication revolution has squeezed our interpersonal communication between large increases in personal communication on one side and mass communication on the other.

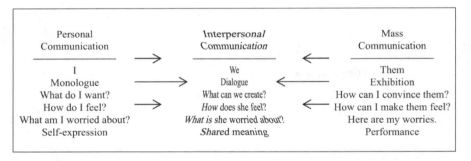

The interpersonal communication squeeze

Our new digital environment encourages personalized communication choices like never before. We can talk when we want, we can talk how we want, and we can talk on devices that cater to our sense of individuality. We can choose an insect ringtone, a disco ringtone, or whether our phone even rings at all. We can get a hot-pink tablet, a jet-black laptop, or a retro desktop computer. We can e-mail, call, and text at all hours. The individual is king of the digital universe, reinforcing an *I*-based approach to communication that squeezes the space for interpersonal communication, where *we*, not *I*, is sovereign.

It's been a struggle for humans to move past their own wants and desires (*I*-based personal communication) and move toward consideration of another person's perspective (*we*-based interpersonal communication) ever since we started interacting centuries ago. But it's harder than ever today because we are pushing back against a relentless tide of powerful products that reinforce the I-based notion that communication is about what's in it for me, on my terms. Let's face it: we aren't lining up at the crack of dawn to get our hands on the latest we-phone.

Interpersonal communication is also under pressure from the increase in mass communication facilitated by the digital revolution. New innovations, like social media, encourage mass communication because now it's just as easy to post a message for 100 people as it is to send the message to a single person.

Yet convenient mass communication masks two fundamental communication realities: adding people always complicates an interaction, and interpersonal messages seldom scale up appropriately for an audience. Communication isn't some new kind of personal app to run. It's our primary tool for creating our lives. And effortless mass communication gives us the dangerous ability to inflict wide damage in mere seconds with our hasty words. It took me over 40 years to build my network, and it's the only one I've got. Today, I can give it a negative jolt in seconds. I now have the asymmetrical power to, instantly and effortlessly, share a viewpoint, reveal a feeling, or post a picture on a social media site that would make everyone in my personal and professional network cringe. Or I can send an e-mail that I'll regret to every contact in my address book.

Mass communication exposes our communication deficiencies for all to see. Before the digital revolution, bad communication habits were easier to conceal; the consequences of failed interactions were more limited, and it was simpler to recover from our errors. Our ancestors never had to worry that their mistakes would bounce around the endless echo chamber of the Internet. The village idiot used to be able to switch villages after saying or doing something stupid. We aren't so lucky.

And we will have plenty of errors on display because communication is, and will always be, unpredictable, frequently difficult, and occasionally baffling. George Eliot pointed out almost 150 years ago that human interaction is even more complicated than chess because each piece on the human chessboard is alive with aspirations, emotions, and desires.[11] Our knights, kings, and queens have minds of their own. The rooks like to endlessly talk over each other, and the pawns are busy texting the queen about trouble with the bishop. But the fact is that we love the crazy old queen, the unruly pawns, and the eccentric rooks—these are *our people*, this is *our life*. And we can learn how to improve our communication with all of them.

The three kinds of collateral damage from the digital communication revolution—the interpersonal squeeze, the embracing of speed and convenience in our interactions, and the inhospitable environment for meaningful communication—are hardly trivial. Unfortunately, they don't represent the largest communication problem we face.

Higher-Order Dreams in a Lower-Order World

Living in a Lower-Order Communication World

More often than I care to admit, I'm guilty of sending a text message, Facebook message, or e-mail to my wife . . . when she's only a few steps away in another room. I sometimes pick the self-serve kiosk instead of the person behind the counter even when there's no line in either place. And I frequently let calls go to voice mail and respond with a text message. I make these communication choices for two reasons: because I can, and because they are easy.

We have become prolific e-mailers, texters, and social media posters. We've so remarkably transformed our phones from devices for verbal communication to platforms for text messages and Internet surfing that some experts predict the death of the phone call; telecommunication companies are rapidly moving from voice-based to data-based subscription plans.[12] A survey of our digital age communication preferences would reveal that for most of us, the majority of our daily communication is quick, expedient, and requires little skill—all attributes of what I call *lower-order communication*.

Lower-order communication is easy and convenient. Practices like sending quick, informational messages; firing off hasty replies; and posting self-expressive thoughts are behaviors that require little skill.

Lower-order communication happens more frequently in *asynchronous* modes of communication where there are lags between messages and responses, like e-mail, text messaging, social media, blogging, tweeting, and instant messaging (which, although it can shrink the time between responses, is still asynchronous). Asynchronous interactions are easier than *synchronous* interactions (where messages are sent and received in real time, like a face-to-face conversation or a phone call), because we choose when to respond to asynchronous messages and because we don't have to integrate immediate feedback cues and other real-time information.

The digital communication revolution didn't just make it easier to send and receive messages; *it also encouraged easy (lower-order) communication*. Dozens of times each day we pick quick and convenient ways to connect over interactions that would require more skill, time, or effort. Because we're busy, and because we can, we take the fast and easy lower-order communication path.

Yet we haven't relinquished our aspirations for higher-order communication. This disconnect is a major problem.

Clinging to Higher-Order Dreams

We want strong and productive relationships. We want to be considered a trusted and valued colleague. We want to come up with the right words when the stakes are high, and we want to effectively comfort or commiserate with a friend in need. These interpersonal aspirations require what I call *higher-order communication.*

Higher-order communication is characterized by thoughtfulness and deliberation; it's harder than lower-order communication because it requires more time, greater competency, and effort. Higher-order communication includes skills like resolving conflict, solving problems, telling stories, arguing effectively, persuading, providing emotional support, generating sales, giving feedback, creating humor, bargaining, and negotiating.

Synchronous communication is usually higher-order because contemporaneous interactions require the constant integration of many verbal and nonverbal cues, like tone of voice and inflection, eye gaze, and facial expressions, and also because we are responding immediately. There is simply more communication "work" to do when an interaction happens in real time.

Higher-order communication involves difficult conversational competencies like trying to understand the other person's perspective, grappling with emerging ideas to arrive at a mutual understanding, and scrambling to comprehend a conversation that's changing with every sentence. Perhaps needless to say, higher-order communication is harder than the lower-order conversational alternative. Higher-order communication skills are more complicated and, consequently, more challenging to acquire, maintain, and improve. It's easier to yell at two feuding coworkers to grow

	Higher-Order Communication Characterized by Thoughtfulness and Deliberation	
Complex Communication Competencies Such as: Conflict Resolution, Persuasion, Emotional Support, Bargaining, Arguing, Feedback, Storytelling, and Humor	**Most Synchronous Communication** Face-to-Face Communication Phone Calls and Skype Real-Time Video Conferencing and Chats	
Simple Communication Competencies Informational Messages Hasty Messages Self-Expression	**Most Asynchronous Communication** E-mail Text Messages Social Media (Facebook and Twitter)	
	Lower-Order Communication Characterized by Speed and Convenience	

Communication Skills — Communication Modes

Higher- and lower-order communication

up (lower order) than it is to help them achieve a workable truce (higher order). Venting your frustrations to a supervisor (lower order) is easier than working with her to alleviate a lingering client problem (higher order). It's easier to resort to cynicism or shock tactics to make your conversational partner laugh (lower order) than it is to say something legitimately funny (higher order). It's easier to mumble an obligatory condolence (lower order) than it is to provide meaningful emotional support (higher order) to a grieving colleague, friend, or relative. It's easier to fire off 10 quick replies to messages in your inbox (lower order) than it is to answer the eleventh message, which requires critical thinking and some kind of a decision (higher order).

Like other complex skills, higher-order communication competencies deteriorate when they aren't used regularly.

I'm not saying that higher-order communication is always better than lower-order communication, or that asynchronous communication is bad and face-to-face communication is good. Plenty of messages can appropriately be handled quickly and easily, and it's entirely possible to send productive messages through both synchronous and asynchronous channels.

The problem is that as the digital revolution unleashed gigantic amounts of information, we coped with the increased load by downshifting almost everything to the most expedient options, even when more thoughtful and deliberate responses were required. Lower-order communication has become the digital age norm, but we still have higher-order aspirations. The result is a growing disconnect between how we communicate (usually lower order) and what we expect our communication to accomplish (often higher order).

The gravest danger of the digital communication revolution is that our higher-order communication competencies are being eroded by ever-increasing amounts of lower-order communication.

The reason we feel like our communication skills have gotten worse in the past few years is because *they have* gotten worse. In essence, we are spending all day playing checkers, while our chess game slowly withers. Some researchers even worry that the underlying biological mechanisms that enable certain aspects of our higher-order communication, like the ability to make and synchronize eye contact and the ability to filter out background noise and tune in to our conversational partner, are in danger of deteriorating from lack of use.[13]

It takes deliberate practice—the cornerstone for developing any kind of expertise—to build and maintain higher-order communication skills and to remain effective in higher-order interaction modes like face-to-face and other synchronous conversations. Expertise also requires focused attention, a challenging precondition in our distraction-prone digital environments. Thanks to the innovations of the digital revolution and dozens of our daily communication choices, we've never been better at checkers. Unfortunately, our communication aspirations keep getting checkmated because the life we really want takes place on a human chessboard that turns out to be anything but quick, cheap, and easy.

But this is no sky-is-falling book. I wrote *Stop Talking, Start Communicating* because this is the *best* time in human history to be a competent communicator. We have remarkable new ways to connect with each other that our grandparents could never have imagined. It's true that it's also incredibly difficult to break free of the gravitational pull of distraction, expediency, self-expression, and excess that characterize so much digital age communication, but we are the masters of our powerful digital devices. We control our communication, and by strengthening our interpersonal communication skills, we can take advantage of the unprecedented opportunities to connect productively and meaningfully with each other.

Some of my advice may sound contrary to what you thought you knew about communication, but stick with me because these counterintuitive messages will help bring your communication competencies into alignment with your higher-order aspirations for your life. New thinking is required because our current methods of communicating aren't working for us. More of the same old thinking will only increase the gap between the communication revolution's potential and the reality we're experiencing.

Each solution-focused chapter of *Stop Talking, Start Communicating* will improve your conversations and add tools to your communication toolkit. This book will help you develop the habits and skills necessary to convert unprecedented connectivity into more of the kinds of productive and meaningful connections you want.

Workable, enduring solutions to the problems of the digital era require a reevaluation of our communication and a sharp reduction in the practices that have caused the digital revolution—for all of its early promise—to make us yearn for the days before our devices stood between us.

1

BACK UP TO GO FORWARD

WE ARE NEGLECTING THREE VITAL COMMUNICATION HABITS

I t was the conversation that he'd been waiting—and paying me—for. After months of work, I was ready to brief my client, a CEO who had asked me to help him determine why his vision for the company wasn't being supported by key executives and employees. I'd spoken with almost every manager, and many employees, in the company, and in the course of those discussions, a clear structural problem and two readily available solutions emerged. I was bringing him very serious, but also very good, news.

The CEO welcomed me into his office, closed the door, and told me how anxious he was to hear my findings. As soon as I began speaking, the CEO's cell phone rang. Apologizing, he looked at the number and ignored the call. Minutes later, after I started sketching out the root cause of his organizational problem, he received a text message. Again, he looked at the screen and ignored it. I continued. So did the interruptions. He never answered a call or replied to a text, but I could see that his eyes—and his mind—were steadily drawn away from the significant organizational issues I was presenting and toward whatever was making noise at his fingertips. Even though the discussion was very important to him, digital distractions prevented him from devoting his full attention to our conversation.

It's not just busy CEOs who struggle to have productive and meaningful interactions. My mom volunteers each weekend with probationers who are required to do community service. In groups of four, they plant trees, weed flower beds, trim bushes, and pick up trash. When break time comes, they all go to a fast-food restaurant and order a drink and a snack. The four probationers sit together, and my mom and the other supervisors give them some space to talk and connect with one another. But instead of a conversation about the morning's work or shared experiences, a connection-stifling pattern usually unfolds: one or two look at their phones, which encourages a third person to put in earphones, and then the fourth person, left with nothing else to do, joins the crowd, pulls out a phone, and stares at the screen. They all miss the discussion that they *could be* having. But it's hard for face-to-face communication—which is difficult, unpredicable, and filled with the risk of errors and slips—to compete with devices that seem to effortlessly give us what we want, when we want it.

Today, most of us struggle to have meaningful interactions because of the power, allure, and distractions of our digital devices. It's easier than ever to gratify our impulses with I-based personal communication and self-expression before an online audience, but harder than ever for meaningful, we-based interpersonal communication. As personal and mass communication exploded in the digital age, essential interpersonal communication skills were left behind. Better digital age communication requires us to retrieve three guiding habits: we need to *listen like every sentence matters, talk like every word counts,* and *act like every interaction is important.*

These three guiding habits can banish the *hyper* from our communication and can restore effectiveness and meaning to the daily conversations that constitute our relationships and our lives.

Listen Like Every Sentence Matters

Perhaps you've seen the setup: a television producer selects someone from a TV studio audience—let's call her Kate—to undergo a psychic reading. Kate has never met the psychic and has no deeply entrenched views about psychics or their abilities. Likewise, the psychic has never met Kate and knows nothing about her until the cameras start rolling.

The reading is broadcast unedited to television viewers. The psychic talks to Kate about her future, punctuating his delivery with questions, comments, and predictions. When the reading is complete, a producer interviews Kate about the experience.

She expresses genuine surprise, noting that while initially she was a bit skeptical, now she believes that the reading was prescient and accurate. Asked if the psychic could be a fraud or a fake, Kate disagrees. He knew too much about her. She believes this psychic has real gifts; he is the genuine article.

Then the producer lets Kate in on the secret: she's been fooled by psychic-buster Ian Rowland, the archenemy of palm readers, mind readers, tarot card diviners, and anyone else claiming to have psychic powers.[1]

Rowland uses a technique he calls cold reading, which consists of asking good questions, making guesses that have a high probability of being correct, and, above all else, listening. Rowland doesn't use magical powers. He just pays careful attention and makes high-percentage predictions based on what he hears.

Yet it feels remarkably like he knows all about a person. And in a way, he does. With the cameras rolling and his professional reputation at stake with every televised reading, he has no choice but to listen carefully.

The first guiding habit for better communication in the digital age is to listen like every sentence matters.

Psychic-busting isn't the only career where listening intently matters. In fact, it's hard to think of a job or activity where careful listening *doesn't* matter, because all interactions—with clients, colleagues, customers, children, and friends—benefit when we pay close attention to the other person.

Listening certainly matters in my consulting work. Most of the solutions to what's ailing a company, group, family, or marriage are within that company, group, family, or marriage. If I listen closely, I can help clients capture their own insights, and those insights can often change a company, reenergize employees, or rehabilitate a relationship.

When people know that they are being listened to about an important matter, their words pour out in a flood. *You would think that these people hadn't been listened to for years.* It may surprise you how well your own employees or colleagues understand the problems and the potential of your company. No matter what kind of organization I visit, I don't find many of the clueless workers who are standard fare for organizational cartoons and television shows. Instead of Dilberts, I find people who have a pretty good handle on what's happening around them, and many of these employees have spent a great deal of time thinking about how to improve work processes.

The same thing applies in my work with people in their personal lives. With rare exceptions, spouses know the state of their marriage. Parents know when they aren't getting through to their kids, and teenagers know when they are driving their parents and teachers crazy. If I listen closely, I can help them crystallize their own workable solutions.

We need to restore the value of listening in our interactions. The digital revolution facilitated hypercommunication and instant self-expression, but, ironically, it made it harder for anyone to listen. There's too much clutter from so much noisy chatter.

Talk Like Every Word Counts

I met Neal just before the start of one of our conference planning meetings. He was going to be our conference operations officer, working with my boss and me to plan and execute a large leadership event at the university where we all worked.[2]

I knew that Neal had a PhD in psychology and that he had won a monthlong trip to Japan in a leadership essay contest. I only had time to ask him a few more biographical questions before I walked to the front of the room and welcomed the attendees. I introduced a few key people, including Neal, and we began working through the agenda.

After the meeting, Neal stayed behind to talk to me.

"Geoff, I want to say thank you," he said.

I told him that I was delighted to be working with him.

"I appreciate the job," he said, "but what I really want to thank you for was your introduction of me."

I tried not to look confused, but I didn't understand why he was thanking me. To me, the introduction was routine: I ran through his credentials, played up his trip to Japan, and spoke favorably about his leadership knowledge. It was standard stuff—background information plus a few kind words. Nothing stood out to me as unusual.

Neal continued. "What I mean to say is that's the nicest introduction I have ever received. No one's ever said things like that about me, and I really appreciate your kind words."

I would later learn that Neal's job at the time was unchallenging and many levels beneath his skills.

A year after the conference ended, Neal landed a job at an East Coast university for twice the pay and 10 times the responsibility. A few years later, when he made another big leap to a top leadership education position at a prominent university, he called to tell me the good news.

Neal said that my introduction of him at our meeting years ago was a turning point in his life. Stuck in an ill-fitting job, he was starting to question his capabilities, but hearing someone put his accomplishments in context convinced him to break free from the position and take bigger risks.

The second guiding habit for better communication is to talk like every word counts. We never know when or how what we say might make a difference. I had no idea, and neither did Neal, that my introduction of him would spur a turning point in his career. None of us knows when a few words of encouragement might prevent someone from giving up on an important project, or when a call from a friend when we need it most reminds us that we aren't alone on this rock.

Sometimes our words come at just the right time, and sometimes words that we think are perfectly timed turn out not to matter. Communication is unpredictable like that. We don't know in advance whether what we say might make a difference, so we need to act like each word is important when we talk.

Act Like Every Interaction Is Important

Careful listening and thoughtful talking—the first two guiding habits—undeniably set the conditions for good communication, but there's a vital third habit. To convert the potential of an interaction into a productive and meaningful connection, we need to treat every opportunity for communication like it's important.

Most cadets don't enjoy the first year at West Point—called

plebe year—and I was no exception. The yelling-prone upper-class cadets, a bone-crushing academic load, and the hot-blooded task-masters in the athletic department made it virtually impossible to relax. So I was delighted when Bernie, a family friend, called to tell me that he was driving up from New Jersey for a home football game on Saturday. Bernie said that he would bring food and that I could invite as many friends as I wanted to come and tailgate before the game.

Bernie was a West Point graduate, which by tradition meant that he could offer plebes in his orbit a no-hassle zone. Even the most adventurous upperclassman wouldn't dare ambush a plebe in the presence of an "old grad."

I took a few grateful plebes to the safe haven of Bernie's tail-gate on Saturday morning, and for two glorious hours, we ate like princes, laughed like jesters, and completely forgot that we were serfs in the military kingdom. Over hamburgers and hotdogs, Bernie told us that plebe year would be over before we knew it and that we were all going to do just fine. He said it so convincingly, and so often, that we believed him. As kickoff time approached, I thanked Bernie for his kindness. He told me that he would be coming back to tailgate for the next football game, and he invited me to meet up with him again. I could scarcely believe my good fortune—I pumped his arm like it was my lucky slot machine.

That season, Bernie attended every home football game, bringing more food each time as my handful of friends gradually turned into a platoon of grateful plebes. Bernie's tailgates were a bright spot in a difficult, and occasionally miserable, year.

Fall turned to winter (which lasted *forever*) and then to a glorious spring that marked the end of plebe year.

A few months into my more leisurely second year at West Point, it occurred to me that Bernie wasn't tailgating anymore. I asked my dad why not.

"Because you're not a plebe anymore," my dad replied. "Bernie's got a lot of other things going on."

"But what about the football games?" I asked.

"Bernie wasn't coming up for the football, Geoff."

Bernie gave up half of his fall Saturdays to provide two hours of stress reduction and pep talks to a plebe in need of both. Once I made it through plebe year, Bernie went back to his life.

How would I have fared at West Point if Bernie hadn't come up for the home football games during my very unpleasant first semester? The question, thank goodness, is irrelevant, because he *was* there and because he acted like there was no place on earth he'd have rather been. Bernie's kindness forged a connection that has continued for over two decades.

Meaningful interactions—the kind that foster authentic connections—don't have to take a lot of time and effort, but they do require *some* time and effort.

Unfortunately, the underlying conditions of the digital age—we're busy, and we can readily access quick, cheap, and easy modes of communication—encourage us to act as if speed and convenience are the most important criteria for how we communicate. Acting like every interaction counts pushes back against the momentum toward ever-quicker and easier interactions.

It takes me more time and effort to talk to a clerk instead of using the self-checkout machine, but the machine doesn't offer the possibility of a brief human connection. There's a danger that walking down the hall and talking to Jim instead of e-mailing him might lead to a time-consuming side conversation about his cats, but what if that conversation points me toward the solution for a long-simmering problem? And it takes time and effort to stay connected with my colleagues from different jobs and projects, with my 95-year-old granddad, and with my young niece and nephew, but what do I lose if we drift apart?

Implementing the three guiding habits—*listen like every sentence matters, talk like every word counts,* and *act like every interaction is important*—will help you be more present in conversations and will improve your digital age communication. But remember that these are guiding behaviors. Don't twist yourself in knots overthinking every syllable and trying to be a perfect communicator (which is an impossible goal because of communication's imperfectability and unpredictability). Instead, use the habits and the techniques we'll look at in the following chapters to become a *better* communicator. That's a goal that's well within your reach and one that will immediately improve your quality of life.

A Life, One Interaction at a Time

The great potential of the adolescent digital age is that there are more ways than ever to communicate and connect with each other. How we manage these newfound communication strengths and mitigate the weaknesses will shape our future.

Higher-order communication modes (or channels) will not always trump lower-order modes. Face-to-face communication is not always a better choice than text messaging or e-mails; they're different communication modes that are appropriate at different times. It makes sense for us to reach for lower-order modes of communication like text messages, e-mails, and social media to manage some of the increasing communication load. Facebook helps me stay in touch with people from all phases of my life. E-mail is unparalleled for swapping data and information. Tweeting is a great way to quickly spread thoughts and ideas. We'll need every implement in our communication toolkit to thrive in the digital age.

Our communication has the potential to provide remarkable benefits, connecting us to others in ways that facilitate innovation, prevent problems, promote sharing, and encourage fruitful exchanges. Research—and our own experience—validates that positive human connections fuel productive and satisfying work and home lives.[3] And effective interpersonal communication encourages the very kinds of interactions that channel good intentions and bring out the best in people, creating the kinds of enduring, fulfilling relationships—creating the kind of meaningful life—at the core of our dreams.

One productive and meaningful conversation at a time, we can transform the underperforming digital revolution from an era of counterproductive excess and frustrating irony into the golden age of communication.

Years ago, I got a call from a CEO on the verge of resigning. His company looked great from the outside—highly profitable with loyal customers—but the company's core staff couldn't get along. The CEO was spending increasing amounts of his time dealing with conflicts that he was unable to resolve.

"I don't know how it got so bad," he said. It used to be fun around here. I miss the times when I couldn't wait to get to work. We've made a lot of money now, and our customers love what we do, but I'd be willing to trade some of that for the days before everyone started fighting with each other."

I asked him what he would change about his organization if he could only fix one thing.

"Can we make it so the people working here like talking to each other again? That would be enough."

Our words are more than enough; they are everything.

Good communication = good relationships = good life.

The company's journey back to productive and meaningful communication required months of work and commitment, but the effort succeeded because almost all the staff members eventually came to realize that *they* were creating the company—and their daily reality—one conversation at a time.[4]

Your life, alive with possibility, begins with your next conversation.

To make the most of our conversations, we'll need to adjust a faulty communication belief that emerged during the digital revolution. We need to expect less from our devices and more from each other. That's how we will add the irreplaceable human touch to the digital communication revolution.

The human touch, of course, is what's been missing all along.

2

INVERT YOUR EXPECTATIONS

EXPECT LESS FROM TECHNOLOGY AND MORE FROM PEOPLE [1]

A sk people what they remember most about the early 1990s and they will likely say the Internet. That was when we first discovered there was something online for everyone. Singles found new ways to meet people. Music lovers found new songs and rediscovered old favorites. It got a lot easier to talk to people on the other side of the world, to find a hotel, to order a book, and to follow the news.

Technological advances ushered in an exhilarating new world, and a steady stream of innovations expanded the boundaries of that world. Our phones got faster, smaller, and smarter, as did our computers. The Internet grew bigger and more sophisticated. Social media sprang up, our contacts swelled out, and the cost of connecting spiraled down. But somewhere along the way, we started drifting away from a people-centered view of communication toward an approach that's increasingly centered on technology.

Twenty years ago, if I'd asked people to close their eyes and think about "communication," they would have likely described conversations, telephone calls, speeches, and possibly handwritten letters (remember those?). If I asked the same question today, the dominant images would probably include tablets and smartphones, text messages and social media platforms. The new additions are mostly asynchronous and *mediated* (that is, sent through a device) modes of communication. They are also ubiquitous. It's emblematic of the shift toward technology that when a marketing expert recently tried to identify the sounds that impacted humans the most, two of the top three noises were from things and not people: the Intel chime, a laughing baby, and a vibrating phone.[2]

As devices have become increasingly prominent in our communication and in our lives, we've shifted toward a more technology-centered view of communication, even though the basic building block of human communication is still, and will always be, two people talking to each other (interpersonal communication).

The problem with a more tech-centered view of communication is that it encourages us to expect too much from our devices and too little from each other. We incorrectly assume that our devices can handle sophisticated communication encounters that they really can't, and we don't give ourselves and other people enough opportunities for the kinds of meaningful human interactions we really want. Until we restore a more people-centered approach to our communication, we will continue to feel unsatisfied and unfulfilled by our interactions, in spite of having the most powerful connection and transmission devices in human history right in the palm of our hands.

Expect Less from Our Devices

A tech-centered view of communication encourages five unrealistic communication expectations.

Unrealistic expectation #1. *Our new and powerful devices have made communication easier.*

Reality. *Communication is as hard as—and maybe even harder than—it ever was.*

In the heyday of the digital revolution, we were lulled into believing that communication was becoming easier because technology made it easier to communicate. But imperfection and misunderstanding can't be engineered out of communication, which involves quirky, emotional, and unpredictable people. And all of our communication can't be easy and expedient, because a great deal of it is complex and requires deliberation.

We communicate for many reasons besides the simple dissemination of information. We persuade, resolve conflict, commiserate, teach, discipline, and motivate. All these higher-order communication functions deteriorate when we prioritize speed and convenience. I create more conflicts than I solve when I approach a thorny interpersonal issue with expediency in mind. I become a less effective teacher when I cram in more information in less time. I'm less helpful as a supervisor when I give my direct reports performance feedback based on hasty conclusions drawn from distracted observations. And so on.

As our new devices facilitated virtually effortless lower-order communication, we mistakenly believed that higher-order communication was also getting easier. In reality, the digital revolution made sending and receiving messages easier, but understanding those messages is harder than ever. This leads to the second faulty expectation.

Unrealistic expectation #2. *Better communication technologies mean better communication.*

Reality. *Our communication capabilities have raced ahead of our communication abilities. Our communication is getting worse.*

We now communicate faster and in a greater volume than people can thoughtfully analyze, understand, and reply. Instead of gaining efficiency, we often fail to rise above the issues and the distractions that our hypercommunication and powerful gadgets bring.[3] New smartphones are trumpeted for their ability to let us talk and surf the Internet simultaneously, even though that is a recipe for miscommunication. All too often, we are texting, typing, and talking right past each other.

Tools that were supposed to make our interactions better have actually fragmented our communication and scattered our mental bandwidth across multiple platforms. If I want to talk to Joe, I have to call his cell phone because he often ignores e-mails. Sam won't reliably answer the phone, but he responds quickly to texts. Cam and Candy are best reached through a Facebook message, and Jim prefers instant messaging.[4]

Today we face the distinct possibility that communication—the very glue of civilization, and a source of primordial connection and enjoyment—is in danger of becoming a net negative in our lives. In spite of the amazing innovations of the digital revolution, our interactions are throwing off more problems, creating more confusion, and generating more trouble than ever before.

Unrealistic expectation #3. *What I want to say is the most important part of communication.*

Reality. *What I want to say is only the beginning of the communication process.*

The digital revolution's promise that we can have communication however we want it, whenever we want it encourages a me-first approach to a process that's fundamentally collaborative. This book is filled with ways to keep ego-centered impulses from distorting our communication, for one simple reason: *What do I want to say?* is usually, and naturally, our first communication thought.

But without expending the effort to consider the other person's perspective—*How will my message impact him?*—we can't transition from I-based self-expression into we-based communication.

Communication scholars have struggled to help people move from a self-centered (personal) to a more collaborative, other-centered (interpersonal) view of communication for over a century. It's normal for our first communication thought to be I-based (*What do I want to say?*), and this isn't a problem as long as the next step is to take the other person's perspective into account and start moving toward mutual understanding and the creation of shared meaning.

Unrealistic expectation #4. *Communicating to an audience doesn't require any special consideration.*

Reality. *Adding people makes communication harder.*

As if the shift from *What do I want to say?* to *How will my message impact him?* wasn't hard enough, the digital communication revolution came along and made mass communicators out of us all. We can send a single e-mail to all of our contacts, reply-to-all whenever we want, and forward messages to everyone we know. It's never been easier for one person to communicate to large numbers of people—just click and go.

Consequently, we've thrown ourselves into mass communicating like it was no big deal, even though it requires us to consider multiple perspectives when we've historically had trouble considering even one perspective in addition to our own. The failure to consider another's point of view or the impact of a message is one reason why so many social media postings feel more like someone is talking at us instead of talking with us. That's *exactly* what's happening.

Interpersonal communication and mass communication are usually different courses of study in academic programs, and for good reason: they *are* different. Having a conversation with your boss is different from addressing the staff. A discussion with one friend is different from a discussion with 200 of your friends.

The most appropriate channel for our message is not necessarily the channel that can reach the most people. Interpersonal messages seldom scale up for an audience without a loss of understanding, because a one-sized message can't easily address multiple perspectives.

Unrealistic expectation #5. *We've communicated once we hit the Send button.*

Reality. *We haven't communicated until someone understands our message.*

While there might be confusion about whether a tree falling in a forest with no one to hear it makes a sound, there isn't any question about whether a message falling on plugged ears or landing in a clogged inbox constitutes communication. If my social media post isn't read, if my e-mail sits unopened under a stack of other messages, or if my text message is overlooked, I haven't communicated.

And although we can technically say that communication has happened when someone reads our message, that's not always sufficient either. We want people to understand our message—not just see or hear it—and we (usually) want them to add their thoughts and ideas. That's the difference between sending and receiving messages and establishing real dialogue, enhancing understanding, and creating shared meaning. That's how we move from hypercommunication to interpersonal communication. The communication we want is only just beginning after we hit the Send button.

A tech-centered view of communication encourages unrealistic expectations that have bedeviled the digital revolution to date. We fell in love with what our tools could do, but we lost sight of the people behind the tools. It's time to turn that around. Our devices don't possess the communication abilities we think they do, and people are capable of much, much more.

Expect More from Each Other

Step 1. Expect More from Yourself

Years ago, I was consulting on an organizational change initiative. It was 3:30 p.m. on a Friday when I heard two senior executives, including the president, yelling at each other so loudly that everyone in the office could hear.

It put me in a tough spot as their communication consultant. Unless you're trying to be heard in a crowded theater or at a Green Bay Packers football game, yelling always signals a communication failure. Conversational escalation—which causes relational damage—was happening. I was in that office to help them reduce their dysfunctional communication, and the boss had just demonstrated that yelling—the timeless marker of failed communication—was an acceptable conversational behavior.[5]

Employees wouldn't have much motivation to improve their own communication as long as one of the most powerful influencers of their corporate culture was screaming at people.[6] My job had just become a lot harder.

Three powerful psychological forces—*reciprocity, social proof,* and *conversational matching*—make modeling the behaviors we desire essential if we want to maintain high communication expectations in our organizations and in our relationships. These mutual behaviors can facilitate—or derail—conversations.

Reciprocity means that our behaviors often trigger similar behaviors in others. For example, yelling at someone makes that person more likely to yell in return, laughter often causes the other person to laugh, and forgiveness and tolerance usually come back to you.

Social proof (also known as the copycat effect or as mimicry) is a psychological process that occurs in uncertain situations. When we aren't sure about appropriate behaviors, we're susceptible to external cues.[7] This is why most people look around a meeting room and quickly adopt the behaviors of others. If everyone is buried in their digital devices, the newcomer pulls out hers; if people are talking to each other, she looks to join a conversation; if the room is silent and people are staring at a written agenda, she'll do the same.

The third force that makes our own behavior so important in setting positive communication expectations is *conversational matching*. In general, humans prefer balanced conversations, where both people talk about as loudly, speak at about the same rate of speed, and pause between comments for about the same amount of time.[8] Talking too quickly puts pressure on the other person to do the same; long pauses between responses are often matched, and loud speaking yields the same in return. Mirror neurons— neurons in the brain thought to influence imitating behaviors— likely play a role in all three of these processes, and research on the matter is ongoing.[9]

If you model appropriate communication patterns, each of these psychological forces—reciprocity, social proof, and conversational matching—will exert pressure on your conversational partner to talk and act like you. This means we have to step up our own communication behaviors to get more of what we want in return.

Step 2. Expect More from Other People

In one of social psychology's most famous experiments, elementary school teachers were told that among a group of incoming students, a small number had scored high on a recently administered intelligence test. The teachers were told which of their students scored in the top twentieth percentile and were thus more likely to "spurt" or "bloom" academically during the school year.[10]

In fact, the names of the "bloomers" had been chosen randomly by psychologist Robert Rosenthal and school principal Lenore Jacobson without regard to their test scores.[11]

By year's end, though, bloomers in the first and second grades were scoring significantly higher than other students on intelligence tests. The teachers' heightened expectations of the students had given rise to a real performance spurt.[12]

The results of this research, not surprisingly, caused a stir in educational policy circles and among scientists. It suggested that at least some of a student's performance is impacted by how a teacher *thinks* the student will perform. The experiment documented what became known as the Pygmalion effect, which occurs when expectations influence actual performance.[13] The Pygmalion effect has an important implication for our interpersonal communication: we can't afford to have low communication expectations. Having high expectations for how we relate to each other isn't wishful thinking—it's pragmatic, self-fulfilling thinking.

The fact is that humans are eminently capable of the kinds of productive and meaningful communication that builds strong relationships and fosters interpersonal connections. To get started, we need higher communication expectations of one another and a more realistic sense of what our communication devices can do. In addition, these four reminders will help us restore a more people-centered communication approach:

1. **Don't let a lower-order interruption trump an ongoing conversation.** The conversation you are having right now is your priority, so don't let your buzzing phone disrupt it. Minimize distractions so you can concentrate, especially when you are engaged in a more challenging higher-order interaction.

2. **Take the other person's perspective.** Perspective taking elevates your thinking from the personal to the interpersonal level. Before you speak or hit the Send button, consider the potential impact of your message on the receiver.

3. **Don't jump up to mass communication inappropriately.** Meaningful interpersonal messages don't scale up to mass channels effectively. Keep interpersonal messages private and direct.

4. **Make understanding a priority.** It's not communication if the other person doesn't understand. Expedient communication, short on thought and on content, often perplexes people.

It's time to expect less from our devices and more from each other. That's how we'll reestablish communication to its rightful place in our lives as less of a burden and more of a gift. And that's how we'll have more of the conversations that build strong and productive relationships.

3

LOSE YOUR "FRIENDS"

IMPORTANT RELATIONSHIPS ARE BEING TRUMPED BY PEOPLE YOU BARELY KNOW

My life of relative comfort came to a screeching halt the day I shipped off to West Point.

After a tough first semester, I returned home to Texas at the holiday break, eager to experience a bit of "normal" life again. But perhaps because I had never perceived my time as scarce before, I had no internal tools to prioritize how to spend my too-brief winter respite. I said yes to almost every invitation that came my way, regardless of whom it came from or what it involved. I played sports I didn't really like with people I barely knew, watched movies I can't remember with distant acquaintances, and ate bland food at mediocre restaurants with people I would never see again.

When my vacation was over, I had a long, gray West Point winter to contemplate how little time I'd spent with the most important people in my life, precisely when I needed those vital relationships more than ever. I was only halfway through my freshman year. The last thing I could afford to do was to destabilize my most stabilizing relationships.

I started to imagine a pyramid, with my most important relationships at the top and other relationships below. It was a simple concept—a critical feature at that point in my life, when I was facing a slew of challenges—but the icon became a remarkably effective and consistent tool that I still use today to clarify who is most important to me and how I need to allocate my time.

I wasn't the only person thinking about those ideas. Right around the same time, Stephen Covey published his perennial bestseller *The 7 Habits of Highly Effective People*. In the book, Covey wrote about a group of people clearing a path through a dense jungle to connect two villages.[1] They threw themselves into the task and worked tirelessly to machete their way through the undergrowth. After a few days, a young boy climbed up the tallest tree to survey their progress. From his vantage point, he could see that they'd become misdirected and that the path they were clearing would not lead to the desired village. The boy yelled down from the tree, "Wrong jungle!"

It doesn't matter how sharp your machete is or how tirelessly you swing it: if the path you're clearing doesn't connect to the right village, you're wasting your precious time. When you devote your time and attention to your most important relationships, you are squarely in the right jungle.

Full-Frontal Attack

The Internet exploded across our lives a few years after I graduated from West Point, and it wasn't long before my pyramid prioritization scheme was under assault.

On the global scale, much of this pyramid smashing was easy to get behind. The free flow of information to closed societies, increased government transparency, and better access to data and information for *billions* of people are things that most of us, save a few dictators, support.

But the Internet didn't discriminate between what should be dismantled and what shouldn't. The digital revolution's remarkable power to erase boundaries and allow instant access to anyone, anywhere, got personal, flattening pyramids and upending hierarchies and relationships for everyone.

The Internet and our digital devices are so powerful that they can easily upend our life's priorities.

This last sentence sounds like a tall Texas tale, but we battle the gritty truth of it every day. Our digital devices, marketed as time-saving tools, have become the robber barons of our time and attention. It's now too easy to send hundreds of marginally important messages, chat with distant acquaintances, and spend hours surfing the web, leaving no time to talk to the people who matter most to us.

No one is immune to the seductive siren song of the digital age. I make my living helping people and organizations establish and make progress toward meaningful goals. I teach classes on time management and peak performance. I write about the dangers of strategic drift in the digital age. But every morning, I still have to fight back the urge to start off my day on someone else's foot by checking my e-mail. And some nights—when I can muster the courage—I review my web browsing history and see that I checked my e-mail more than I needed to and wasted a nontrivial amount of time cruising around the Internet.

A little Internet browsing and a few marginally important e-mails never ruined anyone's life strategy. But we're not really talking about *a little* and *a few*. The Internet inflicts strategic death with a thousand clicks, a thousand seconds of distraction that pile up day after day, supplanting the things we want to do with the things we have a hard time resisting.

The Internet and our powerful digital devices make it easier than ever to swing a high-tech machete in the wrong jungle. A functional prioritization system—even a simple one—that helps you build good relationships by ensuring that the important people in your life get nourishing quantities of your time and attention has never been more important.

The Investment of a Lifetime

Giving your time and your attention to the people who matter most is the investment of a lifetime.

The most comprehensive study of human development and aging, the Harvard Study of Adult Development, began over 75 years ago at Harvard University to explore how people develop over their lifetimes. The study included two cohorts of subjects: Grant study men who graduated from Harvard between 1933 and 1944 and Gleuck study men who grew up in inner-city Boston and were selected for observation from 1940 to 1945. The future president John F. Kennedy was an early participant in the Grant study, and for more than 30 years, George Vaillant was the director and caretaker of this research effort.[2]

Vaillant has published eight books and over a hundred articles based on the study's data.[3] When asked to distill what he had learned from a lifetime of studying the Grant study subjects, George Vaillant replied, "The only thing that really matters in life are your relationships to other people."[4]

The Harvard study will be over soon; many of the subjects are already deceased. In other words, almost all the data are in. And perhaps the most critical finding is this: good relationships = good life.

Time for a Closed-Door Policy

An essential countermeasure against the digital age's ability to give anyone easy access to you begins with identifying the most important people in your life. Use the following pyramid prioritization system, or any system you like, but *have a system* for reserving enough time and attention for your critical relationships.

This pyramid system has four categories, A–D. When you consider where a person fits in your prioritization scheme, imagine that the person is calling you while you are in the middle of an important project or meeting that requires your attention, but one that you could pause if you had to. If you would *always* pick up the call from that person, label the person as part of group A. If you *might* take the call from that person, but you'll always call back as soon as you can, the person goes in group B. If you would let the call go to voice mail, the person is part of group C or D. You'd connect with people in group C within a day, and you'd get back to people in group D whenever you can make the time.

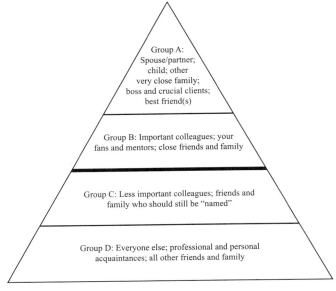

Group A:
Spouse/partner;
child; other
very close family;
boss and crucial clients;
best friend(s)

Group B: Important colleagues; your
fans and mentors; close friends and family

Group C: Less important colleagues; friends and
family who should still be "named"

Group D: Everyone else; professional and personal
acquaintances; all other friends and family

The pyramid prioritization system

Your pyramid prioritization system will situate people into one of four tiers. The top two tiers will have mostly open access to you, and the bottom two tiers won't.

Top of the pyramid: groups A and B—open-door policy

Group A. Always take the call. These are the most important people in your life, emotionally and structurally. This very small group needs—and gets—open access to you. Your spouse or significant other, your children, and your parents probably go here. Your boss and a key client or two are also in this group because of the crucial structural roles they play in your life; their importance in your life and right to claim your time are indisputable. You might also put a best friend and close family members in group A.

Group B. Sometimes take the call. People in group B have good access to you but don't quite make it to group A. You're there for them when they need it, but you monitor this time a little more closely. It usually makes sense to include your mentors and the people who support you the most professionally (your fans) in this group.

Base of the pyramid: groups C and D—not an open-door policy

Group C. Let the call go to voice mail, but reconnect within 24 hours. This category is filled with people you simply can't quite relegate to group D—you feel like they're important enough to be "named," but you aren't going to give them open access. Most colleagues and friends go here, as do many casual friends and extended family members. These people might bump up to group B temporarily if a situation like a specific project or an acute problem warrants it.

Group D. Let the call go to voice mail, and reconnect when you can. Everyone else goes here.

A Pyramid That Works

Once you've completed your pyramid, the question is, *How does your pyramid match up to your life?* The pyramid is what you want; your life is what's *actually happening.* Are there people at the top of your pyramid who are not getting enough of your attention? People at the bottom who are eating up large amounts of time? Make changes to your allocation of time and energy to make your life more congruent with your pyramid.

Notice something else about your pyramid: the majority of the people at the top have been there for years—your spouse, a best friend or two, your closest family, your kids, and potentially even some of the people who mean the most to you at work. *Most of your important relationships are already established, and they are damaged or dismantled at great personal cost.* You can get a divorce, stop talking to a key coworker, escalate a feud with Aunt Betty, or designate a new best friend, but you will be throwing out years—and potentially decades—of your own history each time you do so.

Occasionally, changes like that will be an improvement. Removing yourself from a profoundly dysfunctional relationship with a boss, spouse, coworker, or friend is probably smart. But in an era when we can "unfriend" someone with the click of a button, it's important to recognize that the ease of digitally unfriending masks a significant interpersonal cost.

To put the matter bluntly, most of us are out of time to find a new best friend, and we certainly can't conjure up a new family from scratch. My number of available aunts and uncles is fixed and shrinking. The person I meet tomorrow who becomes my best friend can't get in a time machine and travel back to my youth, to West Point and the army, to my time in academia, or even to my day yesterday. But many of the people already at the top of my pyramid have been through those things with me. These people are my people. They are part of my history and a large part of my life.

My pyramid is not static, though, and neither is yours. Relationships ebb and flow, work roles and bosses change, acute crises requiring time and attention emerge and abate. People move around in any prioritization system over time. Revisit and update your pyramid periodically, especially after significant changes in your life.

Don't mischaracterize the people at the bottom of your scheme as "expendable." Those who are relatively less important today might become more central in your life tomorrow; treating everyone throughout your prioritization system with kindness and decency is both the right thing to do and the smart thing to do, because kindness doesn't create a fraction of the problems that unkindness does. The main reason to prioritize isn't to squeeze people out of your life; it's to make sure that the most important people stay in it.

If you realize that you need to reduce the amount of time you spend with someone at the lower end of your pyramid, do so without fanfare. Most people won't react well to being told that you're going to spend less time with them, so don't tell them. If online messages and interactions are eating up too much of your time, let the unessential ones die on the digital vine, and give yourself more leeway to ignore the e-mails, texts, and Facebook updates from people in the C and D groups.

Doing this may give you chunks of time back without raising any questions. But if someone does ask why you aren't responding to his messages or why you aren't spending as much time with him as you used to, offer an external and valid reason when you have one ("I'm getting crushed at work right now—I just don't have any time," or "Our new baby is taking all my time").

Besides people, what else takes up your time? What keeps you from investing in the relationships that really matter? The best way to determine where your day goes is to keep a time log and, for many of us, to review our Internet history at the end of the day. It's counterproductive to establish a relational prioritization pyramid, enforce it, and then use the extra time to engage in more of the digital age's tantalizing temptations.

But be forgiving with yourself, because some days are less productive than others. Bounce back from a day filled with frequent e-mail interruptions with a morning away from your inbox. Follow 30 minutes of Internet cruising with an hour of meaningful work, and so on. Don't take it personally that the Internet and your digital devices exert pressure on your priorities. They are really good at disrupting all kinds of things.

Trouble with the A Team

Many of the people in the A and B categories can't be moved further down the pyramid. Unless there is a discrete break in the relationship (such as a divorce or a new job), it's very hard to restrict anyone in the A group and many people in the B group as well. Therefore, it can be a major problem if someone in group A or B is constantly dominating your time and attention. I'm not talking about the time you give someone in a crisis or a one-time event, which is understandably and temporarily lopsided. One of the benefits of maintaining a functional prioritization system is that it enables you to facilitate a surge of time and attention when someone you care about is in a moment of need. But *need* is light-years away from *needy*.

See what happens if you give a needy person less of your time and attention, because it's possible that you're enabling some of the behavior. Take the long view and reduce your time and attention to the needy person slowly over a period of weeks and months until you reach a sustainable level.

When we stop and think about it, we know there's more to life than answering e-mails and clicking around on the Internet. A prioritization system will safeguard our time and energy for the important people and activities in our life. From there, we'll need to protect against filling that valuable space with counterproductive communication and incessant chatter. That's the subject of our next chapter.

4

STOP
TALKING

HYPERCOMMUNICATION IS THE PROBLEM, NOT THE SOLUTION

L ong ago when the king of Persia became very sick, doctors told him that the only thing that could cure him was to drink the milk of a lioness.[1] Messengers went throughout the land telling the people that whoever brought the king milk from a lioness would be richly rewarded.

A man named Mordechai found a lioness with three cubs, and after feeding her for days, he was able to carefully milk her.

But on his way to the palace, the different parts of his body started an argument, with each part bragging about how important it was. The eyes said they were most important because they spotted the lioness. The ears said it was they who heard the lioness growl in the tall bushes. The feet bragged that they were able to reach the lioness, and the hands said that they were the most important because they put the milk in the jar.

"I think—," the tongue began. But the others hushed him. "You're always talking," they scolded. "You had nothing to do with any of this."

When Mordechai arrived at the palace with the milk, he was immediately brought before the king.

"Your Majesty, I have brought what you asked for. Here," Mordechai said, holding up the jar, "is the milk of a *baboon* that—."

"What? Baboon milk!" shouted the king. "How dare you mock your king! Take him out and hang him!" the king commanded his soldiers.

Now, the various parts of Mordechai's body were terrified.

The eyes could see the hangman's noose outside the palace. The ears could hear the order for the hangman to get ready. The hands could feel the grip of the soldiers. And the feet knew there was nowhere to run.

"Do you understand now?" asked the tongue. "With one word, and in one second, I can change what all of you have worked so hard to do for days. Which one of us is the most important part of the body now?"

"You are most important," the other parts of the body agreed. "Please help us."

"Your Majesty," Mordechai called out, "I was so anxious for you to receive the milk that I stumbled over my words. This is the milk of a lioness. It will heal you."

Something in Mordechai's voice moved the king to believe him. The king drank the milk and became well again, and Mordechai received a wonderful reward.

But the tongue's reward was even greater. From that time on, all the other parts of the body readily agreed: "The tongue has the greatest power to destroy a person, and also to save him."

Of course, things have changed since Mordechai's day. It's reassuring that we aren't likely to talk with someone who could have us hanged, but in our rush to embrace our exciting new communication devices, we lost sight of Mordechai's time-honored lesson: *our words have the power to save us or to destroy us.*

We've always known that words are *powerful.* They shape the course and quality of our lives and of our societies. Our communication creates and sustains our relationships, and our relationships exert an outsized influence on our overall quality of life. Communication has consequences.

But Mordechai's story also illuminates two other timeless qualities of communication: *imperfectability* and *asymmetry.*

When Mordechai said "baboon" instead of "lioness," he highlighted communication's imperfectability. Errors, slips, and misunderstandings happen whenever people interact. This has been the case since our ancestors started grunting at each other in the cave.

The king's reaction to Mordechai's error illustrates communication's asymmetry. After days of diligent work to secure the lioness's milk, it only took seconds for Mordechai to almost lose his head. Words build relationships slowly, but they can cause damage with lightning speed.

Hypercommunication Hangs Humans Today

In the honeymoon of the digital revolution, we expanded the reach and the quantity of our already powerful words, while forgetting that communication is fundamentally imperfect and asymmetrical. The consequences are troubling, because although more communication doesn't guarantee better communication, it does guarantee more errors because of communication's fundamental imperfection. And asymmetry guarantees that those errors will cost us dearly. Paying less attention to more messages creates more problems than we can readily solve.

Samuel Johnson said over two centuries ago: "If I have said something to hurt a man once, I shall not get the better of this, by saying many things to please him."[2] More recently, research has documented the magnitude of this asymmetry: it takes approximately five positive interactions to overcome the damage from one negative interaction.[3] Our hypercommunicating creates errors faster than we can repair the relational damage.

Healthy, life-enriching relationships at work and at home are built one positive conversation at a time, over months and years. But even our most durable relationships can be seriously damaged in mere seconds of hasty, negative communication. This is why our conversational lodestar must always be to protect our underlying relationships from the asymmetrical damage of our powerful but imperfect words, while we slowly and steadily build up newer relationships with the colleagues, friends, and acquaintances in our lives.

Chatter Pox

The ability to connect with anyone, anytime, anywhere is a blessing of the digital revolution. It's also a curse, because these capabilities encourage us to take advantage of instant self-expression with unremitting chatter.

What we *don't say* is frequently more consequential than the words we choose. As the writer Harlan Miller said, "Often the difference between a successful marriage and a mediocre one consists of leaving about three or four things a day unsaid."[4] The same is true for all our relationships. Less talking provides the vital space that productive and meaningful conversations require.

Space for Listening

During a break at a recent organizational facilitation session I was leading, an employee approached me for a private moment of conversation. He hadn't spoken during the morning session, but he made up for lost time by launching into a spirited description about what he thought was ailing the company and what I should do about it. It only took a few seconds for me to realize that his analysis was significantly different from what my preliminary findings suggested, and while he continued his impassioned discourse, I lined up my counterarguments and what I should say to show him that he was wrong.

Before I launched into that rebuttal, however, I remembered that I was leading a *listening* session. My role wasn't to correct him. I stifled my urge to talk and resigned myself to hearing the rest of his explanation.

As the employee finished detailing his version of the company's troubles, an uneasy feeling came over me: *what if he's right?* The more I mulled over his feedback, the more I realized that my initial assessment was off the mark and that he was correct. During a five-minute break, an employee dropped into my lap the answer to a problem his company had been struggling with for almost two years. And I almost talked right over it.

Less talking provides the space for more listening, and it's amazing what people disclose when someone's listening. Early in my consulting career, I felt a strong urge to try to say something insightful whenever there was a conversational pause. But after more than a few incidents like the one described above, I've become much more interested in the things that I might hear. Less talking made me a much better consultant.

Space for Self-Correcting

Years ago, when I was an army officer, I was given temporary command of an infantry company during a night live-fire exercise. Toward the end of the exercise, a claymore mine malfunctioned and failed to detonate. It fell to me to determine if it was safe to continue or whether we should cancel the rest of the training due to the potential safety hazard posed by the unexploded claymore. It was probably harmless, but under the cover of darkness it was impossible to tell. I consulted with a few people and ultimately chose the safe route.

As word trickled down to the soldiers that the training was canceled, a senior sergeant, who had advised me earlier that the unexploded mine was probably harmless, came running up, shouting and waving his arms to get my attention.

"Sir, I can't believe you canceled the training! That claymore's a dud—it won't hurt anybody!"

To prove his point, he ran out onto the hillside and proceeded to jump up and down on the partially exploded claymore, yelling, "See! See!"

Since he didn't blow himself to smithereens, it was obvious to all the soldiers around us—who mercifully averted their gaze and pretended not to notice—that he was right about the claymore and I was wrong. I was embarrassed, and everything inside me wanted to shout right back at him. But the soldiers on the hill knew both of us well. They knew that I wasn't a clueless officer and that the sergeant wasn't normally prone to drama. We were both having a bad night. So instead of lashing out and making things worse, I choked back my words and started down the hill in silence.

I hadn't gone 50 yards before the sergeant was at my side again.

"Sir, I am so sorry. I don't know what got into me. I should be supporting you and making your life easier—not making things harder. I can't believe I acted like that."

Delighted to have the sergeant, a man I respected and liked, back to his normal self, I told him not to worry about it. We turned and walked down the hill together.

People have a wonderful capacity to recognize and change their own bad behavior and their problematic communication, but only if given space to do so. A quick response to someone else's poor conversational choice enflames the underlying issue and denies the person any opportunity to self-correct. This is like giving a big push in the wrong direction after a single step down an undesirable path. Instead of reflexively responding after a conversational misstep, less talking provides the space for people to recover from their mistakes.

Space for Understanding and Connecting

Quantity is no guarantee of quality in communication. The underlying mechanics of dialogue break down when we cram too many words into our conversations. Too much talking generates confusion, crowds out thoughtfulness, and encourages superficial interactions that are often unproductive, unfulfilling, and error prone.

It's less, not more, talking that often facilitates an interpersonal connection. People require some space to absorb information, formulate their response, and deliver it, and this process repeats many times throughout a single conversation. Too many words create a barrier to understanding.

The more that words pile up, the harder it is for shared meaning to be created, and the more likely an interaction is to fail. Reducing the quantity of our words encourages understanding and increases the likelihood that our conversation might spark a genuine interpersonal connection.

In the movie *A Thousand Words*, Jack McCall is a big talker until he realizes that a magical tree in his yard is tracking his every word. A leaf falls off the tree with every word he says, and when the last leaf drops, both he and the tree will be goners. It takes McCall almost until the final leaf falls to realize that he's talking himself into his grave, but you and I don't have to wait until the relational reaper is tapping on our shoulders to learn the value of less talking.

The Very Bright Side

The good news is that even though the three timeless qualities of communication—powerful, asymmetrical, and imperfect—have worked against us so far, two other timeless qualities of communication—*primordial* and *vital*—give us an opening to rehabilitate, and possibly even transform, the underperforming communication revolution.

Our primordial urge to connect with other people has driven our technological innovations, from the earliest writing to the latest tablet computer. This same innate desire fueled the current communication revolution. We want to connect, and we love new ways to do so. And we keep trying to connect even when some of our interactions go astray. Our primal urge to communicate draws us to people and gives us second, third, and fourth chances to make productive and meaningful connections.

This also explains why the revolution to date has been as frustrating as it has been exhilarating: *connectivity doesn't guarantee a connection*.

Communication is vital to humans in every sense of the word: it's invigorating, dynamic, and essential. It's an understatement, not an exaggeration, to say that communication is an important part of our lives. In fact, *communication is how we make our life.*[5]

This primordiality and vitality is what affords communication resilience in the face of our mistakes, bad habits, and even (some) damage. We want—we need—to communicate. Our most recent conversation might have been awkward and filled with errors, but communication's vitality and our primordial urge to connect pull us forward into the next interaction.

Poor communication is a solvable skills deficit, not a fixed personality type. The fact is that many issues you currently consider relationship problems are actually communication skills deficits. Upgrade your communication competencies and many of your relationship problems will disappear. The ultimate reward for improving your communication is that good communication = good relationships = good life.

We are indisputably in charge of our communication. As the CEOs of our tongues, we can issue an executive order to stop talking. Then we'll need to strengthen two essential communication skills—restraint and containment—to protect our underlying relationships from the asymmetrical damage that's always lurking when two or more people interact.

5

DON'T BE YOURSELF

IT'S AN EXCUSE FOR NEANDERTHAL BEHAVIOR

A few years ago, I watched a colleague blow a major consulting contract by making a joke. After a long day of teaching, the consultant spoke with his point of contact (and paymaster), who complimented him on the training. The client's praise was effusive, and he ended by rhetorically asking how the consultant managed to maintain such a high teaching intensity for so many hours.

My colleague—a very smart and decent man—couldn't resist the words on the tip of his tongue, saying: "That's easy; I'm motivated by money."

The client absorbed the joke like a kidney punch, exhaling audibly. It was clear from his expression that he thought my colleague was making fun of his earnest praise. After a few awkward moments, the client turned around and wandered off. My colleague smacked himself on the forehead, wondering out loud how he could have said something so stupid.

The answer to his question, it turns out, actually involves his forehead.

To simplify a bit of science, our brain has two very different parts—one part is a more primitive, impulse-governed Neanderthal region at the back of the neck, and the other is a more modern and thoughtful executive-functioning area behind the forehead.

Long ago, our Neanderthal ancestors needed a quick-thinking, reflexive brain to navigate a world filled with saber-toothed tigers and club-swinging neighbors, and much of that brain is still with us. But over time, a more modern brain evolved as well, which was capable of reasoning, reflection, and restraint.

The Neanderthal and the modern parts of our brains often operate in tension. For example, when something triggers a negative emotion, the Neanderthal part prefers to club the source of the emotional trigger first and ask questions later, while the modern part suggests that perhaps we should think things through before taking a swing. When a gratifying impulse or urge presents itself—like an urge to say something sarcastic or insulting—our Neanderthal brain will lunge for it, while our modern brain will calculate whether resisting the feeling might be prudent.

Unfortunately, much of the digital era's expedient communication appeals to the Neanderthal's reflexive instincts. We have come to believe that it is our right, as citizens of the digital age, to say what we want, when we want. This is a terrible communication habit to learn. Impulsive and unfiltered communication usually costs our relationships dearly. Saying what we want, when we want isn't modern at all—it's Neanderthal.

It's ironic that our modern devices facilitate the kind of communication that bypasses our modern, reflective brains. Quick communication pushes the act-first, think-later buttons of our Neanderthal brain, but it was the ability to do the exact opposite that helped us out of the cave in the first place.

Now the Neanderthal is at the controls of a sleek new airliner.

Restrain the Cave Brain

Restraint—the ability to *not* say something, even when you really want to—is what distinguishes civilized communication from Neanderthal communication. Restraint also safeguards a thin but vital blanket of civility and politeness that protects most human interactions.

The blanket of civility probably emerged with the earliest advance of human civilization as a way for people to come together and form productive groups, tribes, and societies. Civility required restraint, so that we could live together without clubbing each other over the slightest provocation. Today, conversational civility is reinforced by the underlying desires of people to project a positive impression during an interaction and avoid acts that might threaten either party's self-image, which gives most interactions a healthy dose of mutual politeness.[1]

Restraint is a timeless quality of civilized communication. Ancient ways of thinking suggested that the good life was best achieved through equilibrium, which would enable you to "have control over your emotions, so that you are not battered and dragged about by them like a bone fought over by a pack of dogs."[2]

The ancients were right.

When a lack of restraint jerks the blanket of civility away from an interaction, damage is imminent. Civility and politeness are delicate and easily shredded by impulsive words that infringe on another person's sense of autonomy (like telling someone what to do) or that threaten someone's self-image (like telling someone what he is doing wrong or rendering a criticism).

An example of this happened within my family a few years ago when one of my uncles underwent an angioplasty procedure for stents to open his arteries. He was sedated but aware of what was going on around him. When the display screen showed how clogged his arteries were, the surgeon joked to his team, "Look at the plaque on this guy! I wonder how many sausage biscuits he's had in his lifetime!"

Almost everyone in the room burst out laughing, but not my uncle. The sedation prevented him from saying anything, but his anger at the insult spiked his blood pressure to over 200 and set off alarm bells in the operating room. The last thing my uncle remembers was his doctor snapping at the anesthesiologist: "Quick! Give him more juice!"

The cave brain entertains all kinds of civility-infringing thoughts and impulses. Restraint protects our relationships by preventing those damaging words and deeds from destabilizing our conversations.

Take This Right and Shove It

Not so long ago, there were more structural impediments to our communication. We couldn't afford to talk frequently to people outside our local area code, and it was hard to talk to several people at once unless the conversation was face-to-face. These barriers limited the reach of our communication, but also limited the impact of our communication errors. Our great-grandparents probably didn't have to worry that a 30-second burst of anger might cause 500 of their friends to think they were hotheads. But now we can talk to anyone, anywhere, at virtually no cost. The ability to express ourselves instantly seems like an inalienable right of the digital communication revolution.

If so, it's a right we should consider surrendering. Instant responses far too often are Neanderthal responses, and self-expression isn't all it's cracked up to be. "I was just being myself" sounds harmless, but in a conversation it's often an excuse to indulge in destructive behavior.

The impulses, urges, and emotions that give rise to our Neanderthal behaviors don't have to win—modern humans are capable of exercising restraint in their responses. In the crucial moments between feeling an impulse and acting on it (our response), we hold a conversation's destiny—and possibly the destiny of the underlying relationship—in limbo. Smart communicators don't let their impulses govern their responses.

Feel Better? You Probably Just Messed Up

Failure to restrain your Neanderthal instincts means that your words will all too often trump your goals. What you want to say will destroy what you want to accomplish. The best communicators are able to consistently stifle their immediate, Neanderthal emotional responses. This single action—not allowing your feelings to dictate your words—will impact your quality of life profoundly: *you will get what you want more often.*

Consider the following example:

A coworker always arrives late to staff meetings, inconveniencing everyone and usually causing the meeting to run long. Your goal is to have the meetings start and end on time.

There are probably many things you feel like saying to this tardy colleague: *You inconsiderate idiot, can't you see that we are all here waiting for you, again? Who do you think you are, keeping us waiting every week? What's wrong with you?* All of these thoughts are feelings, though, without a single goal in sight.

Nothing that you *want to say* is going to help your meetings start and end on time. Exacting justice, expressing your frustration, or firing off a snappy putdown might feel good in the moment, but they only put the other person on the defensive and make your conversational goal harder to achieve.

By focusing on what you want to accomplish instead of what you want to say, you're more likely to see options for attaining your goal open up. Perhaps the perpetually late colleague has an unavoidable scheduling issue, and so the meeting needs to start later. Maybe the agenda can be rearranged in such a way that a timely ending is possible. Perhaps you can give the other person a chance to work out the issue on his own. Or you might actually need to have a direct conversation with the tardy coworker. None of these possibilities can be achieved—or even approached—if you say the first thing that pops into your mind.

I'm not suggesting that feelings don't matter. But I am suggesting that we choose *how* and *when* we address our emotions. A deliberate conversation with someone about why you feel angry with him, for example, is completely different from reacting spontaneously in anger.

Exercise restraint and communicate with thoughtfulness, because the person in front of you is more important than the feeling inside you. What you want to accomplish is more important than what you want to say.

The choice between acting on your primitive instincts and listening to your communication conscience—your internal voice of restraint and thoughtfulness—is the difference between success and failure. It's the difference between civilized and uncivilized communication.

Five actions can strengthen your restraint and build your communication conscience:[3]

1. **Practice not talking.** Think of restraint as a muscle and resolve to make it stronger through daily practice. If you consciously try to choke back unhelpful comments and ill-chosen words, your restraint muscle will, over time, grow to become a prized communication asset.

2 . **Delay your responses.** Restraint inserts itself between what you feel like saying and what you actually say, so focus on consciously enlarging this area. Just a few seconds can mean the difference between a measured response and a destructive one. If you are worried about your ability to restrain a response, remove yourself from the situation.

3 . **Resist the urge to prove someone wrong.** Few things test our restraint more than holding our tongue when we're right about something. Avoid the temptation to say "I told you so" or draw attention to your conversational partner's errors. Being magnanimous is better for your underlying relationship than being right.

4 . **Eliminate witty comebacks, put-downs, and insults.** Put-downs and witty comebacks may feel good to you for a few seconds, but they cause a lot of heartburn down the line. Insults are the antithesis of smart communication because they gain you nothing but can potentially cost you a great deal. When you feel a witty comeback sizzling in your head, restrain yourself. Send the urge to the corner and put a dunce cap on it.

5 . **Give yourself credit for the things you don't say.** Restraint isn't flashy or glamorous, but it won't blow up your relationships or torpedo your goals. Give yourself credit for all the trouble that you avoid, for all the words that you choke back, and for all the dustups that you steer clear of. These invisible accomplishments will be some of your most important communication achievements.

Exercising restraint doesn't mean that you'll become a robot, and unfortunately it also doesn't guarantee that you'll be perfect at resisting urges. Occasionally, your impulses or emotions will overpower your restraint, and damaging words will tumble out. When this happens, nothing beats a quick and sincere apology. People usually accept timely apologies for all but the most egregious of verbal transgressions. We'll discuss apologies more in Chapter 10. For now, when a lack of restraint gets you in trouble, have an apology at the ready.

ABC: Always Be Containing

Restraint stops trouble before it happens. But when restraint falters and a conversation escalates because either you or your conversational partner gave in to your Neanderthal instincts, *containment* prevents the damage from becoming insurmountable and protects the underlying relationship. Because words can damage relationships quickly, but relationships can only be built slowly (asymmetry), containment is an essential tool to ensure that you don't unwind years of goodwill in seconds of a hasty, damaging conversation.

Containment stops conversational escalation, which is crucial because *all relational damage happens when conversations escalate*. That's no exaggeration. Conversations characterized by mutual restraint don't damage relationships; only escalated conversations do.

As conversations escalate, two harmful things can happen. First, words become more hostile, negative, and hurtful, transforming small disagreements into epic arguments. Second, it becomes increasingly likely that someone will pursue hazardous conversational tangents. Words turn spiteful, and topics that are best left untouched come flying out of the darkness.

Research suggests that containment and containment attempts are hallmarks of strong and successful relationships.[4] On the other hand, escalating words—regardless of justifications and provocations—produce dueling dialogues that are likely to end in disaster. And the root issue of the conversation, which may have originally been quite manageable, becomes more difficult to resolve as positions harden.

After a destructive conversation, people often look back and wonder, *Where did that come from?* It's no surprise they didn't see it coming—it *wasn't* coming until the conversation escalated.

Remember this crucial point: *only escalating conversations dismantle relationships.* If you can restrain yourself from yielding to your Neanderthal urges in the first place, you'll prevent a great deal of harm. When restraint fails, containment is there to halt the escalation and limit the damage.

Containment is the lifeline thrown to a conversation taking on water. To adapt a phrase from the movie *Glengarry Glen Ross,* remember your ABCs and *always be containing.*[5]

Conversational Escalation and Containment at Work

Jim: Hi, Bob. Do you have a minute to talk about the Anderson project?

Bob: Sure, what's up?

Jim: I'm worried that the boss isn't going to like the report because the market analysis is a bit underdeveloped. (Root issue)

Bob: I'm not sure I agree with that. There's plenty of material in there. And the boss is mostly concerned about the financial numbers, not the marketing stuff.

Jim: Well, I'm still thinking that we should beef up the marketing section, just to be sure.

Bob: Go ahead. I don't have any more time to adjust the report, and besides, I disagree that the boss is after marketing material.

This is a critical moment in the conversation. Bob has opened the door to escalation, but at this point in the conversation, not much damage (if any) has been done. Jim can choose to contain here and walk away before it gets any worse, or Jim can reply to Bob's last statement and escalate. Alas, Jim chooses to escalate.

Jim: Listen, man, even if I am wrong about this, you could stand to be more receptive. This is a team project. This is why people don't want to work with you.

Jim's lack of restraint and subsequent tangent escalates the conversation. At this point, anyone could make a containment attempt, but neither person does.

Bob: That's ridiculous. And being part of a team isn't license for you to waste my time or add irrelevant material. I've been working on this project a lot longer than you, and I think I have a better sense of what's required. Your input has been misguided from the start. (Continued escalation)

At this point the conversation is almost completely disconnected from the root issue, and relational damage has almost certainly been done. And the archrival of successful conversational containment—emotional responses—is on the loose. Many conversations would continue to escalate from here, piling on the damage. It takes a lot of self-control to contain at this point, but this is what Jim and Bob do next. It's time to stop the damage, redirect the conversation, and get out of it.

Jim: Whoa! Let's let the boss be the judge of my input. I can't see any harm in strengthening the marketing section, just in case. I'll add a couple pages to the marketing part, and that will probably make me feel better. Sorry about getting you upset. (Multiple containment attempts and a redirection to the root issue)

It's smart that Jim absorbed the insults and contained the conversation here, although the insults would never have materialized if Jim had been able to restrain himself at the beginning of the conversation.

Bob: Okay, fine. Look, I have an old marketing section from the Gatorville account that I'll send to you. Just replace Gatorville with Anderson, and we won't have to create anything new.

Containment from Bob and resolution of the root issue give Jim the perfect chance to exit the conversation.

Jim: Great, thanks a million. (Jim sticks out his hand, they shake hands, and Jim exits.)

In this conversation, the damage was contained, but not before insults were exchanged. Containment was the best solution possible after restraint failed, but initial restraint could have prevented the damage from happening in the first place.

ABC Meets DR. E

Containment has three steps: *deescalate*, *redirect*, and *exit (DR. E)*. These three steps limit the damage from unrestrained words.

Containment Step 1. Deescalate

Conversations, be they computer mediated or face-to-face, can be deescalated by any action (or inaction) that drops a conversation's intensity level. There are five ways to deescalate. Use them in any combination to restore conversational civility:

> ➤ **Stop trying to score points or add new material.** Shut down the voice inside your head that's telling you to fight back. Retaliation will only increase the conversation's intensity. Forget about all the good counterarguments you can make. Stop looking for holes in the

other person's reasoning, errors in his logic, or faulty assumptions that you can counter. Protect the underlying relationship.

➤ **Take a break.** Breaks are incredible containment devices, but they are woefully underused. You can stop the momentum of an escalating conversation in its tracks by asking for a pause to allow emotions to moderate and to provide an opportunity to reset a heated conversation.

➤ **Apologize for something.** Apologies are great deescalation tools. You can apologize for the escalation itself ("Look, I'm really sorry that our discussion got heated"), for a particular portion of the conversation ("I'm sorry that I brought up an irrelevant issue"), or for virtually *anything* that doesn't sound too contrived or patronizing.

➤ **Offer a relevant compliment.** Compliments can't be irrelevant ("Your kids are so smart" or "You look really good in those pants"). Instead, say something about some portion of the other person's thinking or logic that fits the context of the conversation ("I hadn't thought about it like that; that's a good observation"). Any touch of kindness is a reminder that there is an underlying positive relationship tangled up in the temporary escalation.

➤ **Acknowledge a positive intent, emotion, or feeling from the other person.** Tell the other person you appreciate her willingness to tackle a difficult issue or that you respect her concern about the issue. Almost anything positive that you can find in the conversation or in her approach to the conversation will probably work ("I appreciate how much you care about solving this issue").

In theory, asynchronous digital devices should make deescalation easier, because the built-in lag between a message and our need to respond should function as an organic firewall. In practice, instead of making good use of the natural pause, we too often cast aside the containment advantage and reply quickly.

Consider the upsetting e-mail you receive from a coworker: "I don't think your report is ready to send to the client." Instead of collecting your thoughts, you immediately call him, or you fire off an escalating reply: "I did the best I could with the poor data and analysis you sent me." Or you get a chastising text message from your spouse: "U 4got 2 feed dog again," and you shoot back: "H8 that fleabag anyway."

People say all kinds of counterproductive things when conversations escalate. But the good news is that if you ignore unhelpful comments and focus on containing and returning the interaction to civility, your conversational partner will often self-correct. Containment gives the other person an opportunity to get his modern brain back into the conversation, which sometimes requires a bit of patience and time. Don't be surprised if you end up containing five unhelpful comments before the other person corrects and civility is restored.

Anything that puts distance between an emotion and a response, whether in face-to-face conversations or digital ones, is a natural deescalation ally. Time and space help keep the Neanderthal at bay.

Containment Step 2. Redirect

The key to successful redirection is gently bringing another person back to the root issue without making her feel like you're trivializing her concerns or trying to control the conversation. (If there is no root issue—nothing to solve or no actual substance behind the escalation—you can move to containment's final step and exit the conversation.)

Redirect your conversation away from all escalations and unhelpful tangents. For example, if a coworker believes that your accounting reports are inaccurate (the root issue), but the conversation escalates into criticisms about your inattention to detail in general (a tangent), you might redirect by saying: "Okay, I want to fix this. Please tell me how I can improve my accounting reports." Or "I hear you. Let's figure out this report so we don't have trouble again."

Containment doesn't take away your voice or sacrifice your ability to wrestle with a root issue. You may need to ignore unhelpful words (like the comments about your carelessness in the example above) to successfully deescalate, but once the conversation is contained, you and your partner can work on the root issue civilly.

In a perfect world, it would be preferable (and easier) to exit a conversation immediately after successfully deescalating it, skipping the redirection process entirely. After all, whatever triggered the initial flare-up is likely to be still lurking in the background. However, here in the real world, redirection is often necessary, because it can be difficult to get the other party to walk away from an escalated conversation. People assume that an escalated conversation is an important conversation, and in some ways this is true: an escalated conversation *has become* important, even if the initial issue was relatively minor. Consequently, it's wise for you to treat an escalated conversation as important and to redirect to the root issue after deescalating. Just be careful, because containment is never permanent, and escalated conversations leave smoldering embers. You may need to deescalate and redirect multiple times in a single discussion, tamping down the conversational flames as they flare up.

At some point, you will have addressed the root issue, determined that there isn't one, or concluded that the conversation is too hazardous to continue. All roads lead to a conversational exit.

Containment Step 3. Exit the Conversation

Exits matter. People pay attention to how conversations end, and, especially after an escalation, they want to know that you aren't running away from their concerns. There are many ways to exit an escalated conversation appropriately, including:

> ➤ **Give the other person an opportunity for closing thoughts.** Ask, "Is there anything else we should discuss?" or "Any other thoughts?" Use your judgment here—if you think that giving the other person the last words might reopen sensitive parts of the conversation and undo your containment, then summarize the discussion and offer last words instead. But if you sense that the emotions involved with the escalation have dissipated, offering last words to the other party can send a strong signal of trust and goodwill.

> ➤ **Offer a plausible reason for why you need to leave.** Real, external reasons why you need to conclude a conversation make exits easier. Say something like "I'm late for work," "I have to pick up the kids from school," or "I'm on a conference call at three o'clock," and then make your exit.

> ➤ **Ask the other party if you can set the conversation aside for a period of time.** If you are unable to resolve the root issue, ask if you can pause the conversation and return to it later. Let your conversational partner determine how long the pause should be—your main priority is simply to discontinue the discussion and allow for a conversational reset. Set a time to come back to the discussion and honor it.

Keeping the Revolution Out of the Cave

Our digital devices have enormous potential, but it's up to us to add the human touch. Technology will pass along whatever we want: straight data, disjointed messages, good ideas, trivial e-mails, or expressions of care and concern. Our communication, enhanced as never before, has the potential to connect us together in a way that makes work—that makes life—productive, meaningful, and fulfilling.

We can't afford to let our shiny communication tools become a cover for Neanderthal behavior, carrying us back into the cave under the paradoxical banner of progress. Civilized communication—conversations characterized by mutual restraint and by containment when restraint falters—encourages the meaningful human connections we desire.

Next up, we discuss one of the most stealthily effective skills to have in our communication toolkits.

6

PLAY
DUMB

DON'T PIN THE TAIL
ON THE DONKEY

Most of us are familiar with the image of the *see no evil, hear no evil, speak no evil* monkeys with their hands covering their eyes, ears, and mouths. The image, called the three wise monkeys, can be traced to a seventeenth-century carving at the Toshogu shrine in Japan. The maxim probably existed much earlier, as a similar sentiment was included in a second-century collection of Confucian aphorisms: "Look not at what is contrary to propriety; listen not to what is contrary to propriety; speak not what is contrary to propriety; make no movement which is contrary to propriety."[1]

The durability of the maxim attests to its timeless wisdom. Seeing, hearing, and saying (or typing) no evil—what we call *playing dumb* in this chapter—is more necessary than ever in the digital age, when we are doing so much more communicating, than it was when Confucius set down the advice nearly 2,000 years ago.

73

Why Playing Dumb Is Smart

Seldom does a week pass without a politician, celebrity, athlete, or business leader making the news for saying something stupid that's broadcast all over the land.

While we may outwardly chuckle—or wince—at the gaffes, many of us also secretly sympathize, because similar things have happened to us, though mercifully on a smaller scale. We've sent reactive messages and immediately realized our mistake. We've left imprudent voice-mail messages when we were angry that we'd like to erase. And at some time we've all said something so preposterous that we leave our conversational partners scratching their heads or looking down at their feet.

The digital age exposes those dumb statements mercilessly, while simultaneously making it harder—and sometimes impossible—to erase the reminders of our ill-chosen words.[2] And the speed and expedience of digital communication encourage us to create more messages with less thought and preparation, practically guaranteeing that we will transmit more faulty messages that we want to take back. What used to be a rough draft, with all its errors and omissions, is now a final copy, because we don't allot the time for revision and reflection.

Research, and our own experience, suggests that people often feel less inhibited when communicating in asynchronous and device-mediated ways and that those messages often contain more sensitive details and more forceful thoughts and opinions.[3]

As inhibition falls, the need to emulate the three wise monkeys rises. When you're faced with a message that probably should never have been sent, the best way to react is to play dumb.

Playing dumb means that, for the benefit of your relationship, you quietly act like you don't see or hear something. Playing dumb is a versatile and effective way to prevent relational damage. It's a smart and humane communication strategy that benefits you, the person in front of you, and the underlying relationship.

Playing dumb benefits your conversational partner by allowing her to recover from ill-conceived words and messages. As we've discussed, people often self-correct if we give them the space to do so. When you don't immediately respond, you provide that opportunity for a person to voluntarily come back with "That's not quite what I meant" or "I can't believe I just said that."

Playing dumb benefits your underlying relationship by deescalating a situation and allowing hasty words to disappear without comment. You'll stop conversational escalation before it starts.

And playing dumb benefits you by allowing you to ignore statements you don't want to acknowledge, like when a colleague shares shocking but irrelevant gossip. Not every comment deserves recognition, and not every topic merits a discussion.

Do you have an important client who loves to share conspiracy theories? A boss whose politics are to the right of Attila the Hun or to the left of Wavy Gravy? A coworker who makes inappropriate comments about other people in your office? These are all excellent candidates for playing dumb.

Playing dumb can keep you out of conversational quicksand—and mud—and let words and topics you want to avoid die an early and merciful death.

Not So Easy

Playing dumb sounds simple: just don't react. And it yields compelling relational benefits. So why do we play dumb only a fraction of the times we should? Because it's hard to override our instincts—and our desire—to respond. There's a reason why the three wise monkeys were emblazoned on the Toshogu shrine and why Confucius thought it was important to render his timeless advice.

Playing dumb requires unusual intelligence.

Playing dumb is challenging for many reasons, but the most obvious is because we feel obligated to respond when spoken to or to reply when we receive a message. As conversations pick up a rhythm, or as our inbox stacks up, we feel increasing pressure to respond when it's "our turn" (so much so that *turn* is the word used in communication research to describe when people speak in conversation).

Imagine that you're talking face-to-face about a project with a coworker named Jack. The interaction has been productive, but at the next turn in the conversation, Jack says: "We sure haven't got much help on this project from Jill. I don't know how she keeps her job." And then he stops. It's your turn.

You don't exactly think Jill is the employee of the month, but you aren't interested in mudslinging either. Still, the momentum of the conversation propels you toward responding ("I agree," or "She's really a piece of work," or "You're right").

Conversations have a trajectory that moves people along, and the force is tough to stop. Most of the time, this flow facilitates communication and can explain why you feel a reflexive urge to respond to Jack's comment. If you can overcome that, silence is the most common and effective way to play dumb, but sometimes it's easier to reply neutrally or ambiguously instead. You could say to Jack "I see," "Okay," or "I understand why you feel that way" in a response that doesn't explicitly affirm his statement. Alternatively, you could redirect to the conversation's main point after hearing a comment that should be ignored: "The project's been going well up to this point, Jack, and I think we should focus on incorporating the client's feedback next."[4]

The important thing is to move the discussion away from the offending words. Silence, neutral responses, or redirection can often get a conversation back on track. It's also possible that your silence, ambiguity, or redirection will clue in your conversational partner on the kinds of comments that stifle conversation. If this knowledge leads to better dialogue in the future, playing dumb will have delivered both short- and long-term benefits.

The second reason why we don't play dumb as often as we should is a bit embarrassing: *we don't want to.* We get a twisted satisfaction from holding people to their dumb words. A coworker says something about a client that's so outlandish—and usually counter to what we believe—that we pounce on the statement. During Thanksgiving dinner Uncle Billy demonstrates an eye-watering insensitivity to people from other parts of the world, and you carve him up like the turkey. A colleague who's having a bad day spouts off about "how things really work in business," filling his polemic with half-truths, speculation, and kindergarten-level reasoning. Instead of letting him harmlessly have his say, we break out the proverbial red pen and start correcting his errors.

Another reason we don't play dumb is that we like closure. We don't want to leave a conversational thread hanging in the air, because humans naturally sense that something is amiss when conversations are incomplete. We scramble to find endings. You've probably had the experience of wondering when you could stop responding to a text message, an e-mail, or a social media posting. When, exactly, does the conversation end? Do I have to say good-bye after Jill says good-bye, or is the conversation already over? After Jim says "You're welcome" to my thank you, do I have to write him back, or is the conversation already over?

The same hunt for closure happens in synchronous (face-to-face and phone) conversations, but usually with more cues to help us. When is it time to move on at a cocktail party? How can we leave the boss's office after the discussion is basically over but the boss is still talking?

We also don't like playing dumb because, well, we don't want people to think we're *actually* dumb. If we don't respond to an off-color joke from a colleague who just revealed himself to be (at least) 1 percent perverted, 1 percent bigoted, or 100 percent idiotic, will he think we didn't get it? But ignoring words that are pointless—or worse—is anything but dim-witted.

Finally, playing dumb is hard because conversational silence can make everyone uncomfortable. Playing dumb requires an appreciation, or at least a tolerance, for pauses and silence that most of us don't naturally have. Next time you're talking with a friend, start adding pauses (count to four) in the conversation and see how that makes you feel. See how your friend reacts. Most likely, you'll feel uncomfortable, and your friend might wonder if you put the wrong kind of mushrooms on your pizza.

You can engineer that discomfort to work in your favor. Making your conversational partner notice something unnatural—the silence—might make him think about what's happening and self-correct or switch topics. A few seconds of silence, and a bit of conversational discomfort, can often restore sanity to a temporarily dysfunctional interaction.

Playing Dumb for Dummies

Five rules will help you play dumb more effectively:

1. **Hide any nonverbal signals that you are playing dumb.** Put on your best poker face. Playing dumb is considerate when it's done discreetly, but it's embarrassing to the other person when it's overt. So while you're being silent, also keep your eyes from rolling at whatever ridiculous things you've just heard.

2. **Understate your dumbness.** Be inconspicuous. If you oversell your dumbness by acting like one of the Three

Stooges, being totally clueless or befuddled, you'll draw unwanted attention to your actions, or you may cause the other person to double down on her unproductive words. Dumbness works best when you subtly allow the other person to take advantage of the gap in the conversation to walk back from her ill-advised words.

3. **Don't add anything substantive if you have to talk.** It's easiest and best when your silence and intentional gaps provide enough room for someone to self-correct. But you can play dumb and still talk, as long as you don't add anything substantive to the conversation. Use neutral continuers like *um-hum, I see, okay,* or *I hear you.* There's a danger that the other person will hear your neutrality as a tacit approval of his statements, so use them selectively and exert your right to remain completely silent when you hear something so offensive that you don't feel comfortable being neutral. If your conversational partner asks about your lack of reaction, you can say you have nothing to add, politely request a topic switch, or just start talking about something else.

4. **Resist the urge to prove someone wrong.** Unless something crucial hangs in the balance, if you hear someone misquote a statistic, mangle a story, or make a logical error, don't whip out your smartphone and start searching the Internet to prove her wrong. And when someone lays a goofy conspiracy theory or profoundly loopy worldview on you, don't treat it as your moral obligation to set him straight. Playing dumb means letting go of the need to be right about everything.

5. **Don't play dumb too often.** There's a line between playing dumb for relational harmony and playing dumb because you are in denial about a clear and present relational problem. If you find yourself playing dumb fre-

quently, it may be a warning sign of a larger issue that you need to address. Fundamentally, playing dumb involves a trade-off: we sacrifice part of a conversation in the short term in order to preserve an underlying relationship. Don't misuse the technique to avoid important relational issues. There are other communication tools to help you handle relationship problems.

You might find that it's beneficial to play dumb more consistently with bosses, key clients, and important colleagues, where you have less leverage to alter their behavior. You might also choose to play dumb with older relatives (it's usually impractical to pressure people to change toward the end of their life) who have a penchant for saying ill-advised things that drive you crazy but don't really harm you. In these cases, your long-term strategy might be to listen and comment when necessary, without adding anything substantive, or to change the underlying conditions to limit the instances of problematic communication. If a key client tends to make off-color jokes after a couple of happy-hour cocktails, start inviting him to breakfast instead. Or if Aunt Sarah can't resist criticizing your housekeeping every time she comes over, try to visit at her house, instead.

When playing dumb succeeds, it usually results in either a topic switch or a conversational exit. If playing dumb fails, try to exit the conversation or change topics by talking about something else or circling back to an earlier (and inoffensive) thread in the conversation. Alternatively, you can ask for permission to switch topics ("Can we talk about something else?"). People will often get the hint or simply acquiesce to your request.

Playing dumb illustrates the power of *communication in its absence*. We exert a profound influence on interactions with what we don't say, type, or forward.

Playing dumb occasionally is a gift—a break—we give to our relationships. In today's communication environment where speed routinely trumps deliberation and where restraint is often abandoned by the desire for self-expression, we need all the breaks we can get. Instead of pinning the tail on the donkey, play dumb and give him an opportunity to self-correct.

Playing dumb is one of the smartest, and most altruistic, moves in your communication toolkit.

Now it's time to take a look at another communication tool, questioning, that you probably don't think about very often. Unfortunately, it shows.

7

QUESTION YOUR QUESTIONS

MANY QUESTIONS MAKE CONVERSATIONS WORSE

For the next week, watch what happens any time you or someone else asks a question during a conversation. You'll quickly find that questions are not always neutral. They make some of your conversations better, but questions make a surprisingly large number of your conversations worse. Like an incredibly talented but wayward cousin, a question has the potential to do a lot of good, but it will often underperform and disappoint instead.

It's not always easy to divine another person's intent behind a face-to-face query, and the task is much harder in the digital age of mediated and asynchronous messages where we lack nonverbal cues and the ability to gather immediate feedback.

Even "simple" inquiries can go awry. "Is this the most recent report?" or "Did you call Jim in accounting about this?" can cause trouble if the other person thinks there's a criticism behind the query. Many household arguments have been started by questions like "Did you let the dog out?" or "Are your parents coming to dinner?"

The truth is that some of what you currently consider relationship problems probably reflects your underdeveloped questioning skills. Faulty questions contribute to many conversational failures and can add anxiety, defensiveness, and ill will to interactions. Good questions facilitate understanding, lubricate conversations, and promote learning. They bring people together, while faulty questions push people apart and can lead to communication breakdowns.

If you improve your questions, you'll improve your relationships. And if you improve your relationships, you'll improve your life. That's a powerful incentive to upgrade your questions.

Gaston de Lévis said over 200 years ago that we should "judge a man by his questions rather than by his answers."[1] Unfortunately, our questioning skills today wouldn't stand up to that kind of scrutiny.

Most of us are poor questioners, because questioning is a higher-order communication skill that we haven't taken seriously for centuries. The days of Socrates masterfully using questions to lead a conversation are long past, and the digital age is not very conducive to thoughtfulness or deliberation—two prerequisites of effective questioning. Good questions take time to construct, but bad questions emerge instantly. Many of your least helpful thoughts come out of your mouth in the form of questions.

The ease with which we can turn to the Internet to answer virtually any question we ask lulls us into thinking that questions are simple and that answers exist to meet our needs. We request information, and someone (or something) else provides it. We have no further responsibility in the exchange. But people aren't search engines, and expedient questions aren't always helpful.

In general, the more we query simply to indulge our personal, I-based cravings to get an answer, to hammer home a point, or to satisfy a narrow, personal curiosity, the more our questions are likely to stifle dialogue. The more we focus on what we can learn from or about another person (a we-based perspective), and the more our queries reflect a broad curiosity about the person or topic we're discussing, the more our questions will fuel meaningful conversations.

Help Your Questions Live Up to Their Potential

The most effective way to improve your questioning skills is to stop asking faulty questions. Here are the most common types of faulty questions to avoid.

Rhetorical or Unanswerable Questions

During the vice presidential debate in 1992 with Al Gore and Dan Quayle, Admiral James Stockdale, the running mate of independent candidate Ross Perot, began his opening statement with two questions that would quickly become famous: "Who am I?" and "Why am I here?"

Stockdale answered his own questions, but so did the American public and the late-night comedians. Some responses were brutal, including an infamous *Saturday Night Live* skit where an actor playing Ross Perot desperately tried to leave Stockdale by the side of a deserted road.

Lost in the clamor over Stockdale's debate performance was who, in fact, he was, including his impressive legacy of public service. Admiral Stockdale earned the Medal of Honor as the POW leader of the "Hanoi Hilton" prison camp during the Vietnam War, but when he died in 2005, his two debate questions continued to receive top billing in his obituaries.[2]

Questions that can't be answered, such as rhetorical questions, create conversational hazards by producing a bind between a person's perceived obligation to respond and the fact that she can't.

People react to this dilemma in many counterproductive ways. They may lash out in frustration if they feel trapped—most of us have been surprised by a hostile reaction to what we thought was an innocent question. Other times people find creative answers to questions that were supposed to go unanswered. Ask "Why do I put up with this?" and you might hear "Because you can't do any better!" The question "What's the point of talking to you?" might be answered with "Don't bother, I'm ignoring you anyway!"

Don't ask a question if you really don't want an answer. And be wary of continuing a line of inquiry if it isn't turning up useful responses. You aren't learning anything, but you might be steadily ratcheting up the pressure for a damaging response.

Ask questions with care. If people are willing to pounce on the faulty questions of a war hero, they will make mincemeat out of yours.

Unwanted Questions

There are some questions that people just don't want to answer. These questions might be perceived as too personal ("How much money do you make?"), too embarrassing ("How did you lose the Gatorville account?"), or inappropriate ("Where'd you get that rash?"). Consider whether you're asking for too much information before posing your question, and be aware of cues that you might be pushing into sensitive areas. A sudden urge by your conversational partner to look down and shuffle his feet probably indicates that he'd rather not talk about Gatorville, his salary, or his rash.

Leading Questions

Leading questions give away the "right" answer that you're looking for. "Isn't this a good idea?" "Don't you think that Gatorville is a terrible client?" and "Isn't it obvious that Aunt Bessie is mean and nasty?" Try persuasion instead of leading questions. You may not get what you want, but your conversational partner will probably appreciate the more direct approach.

Loaded Questions

Loaded questions are poorly disguised criticisms that don't lead to productive conversations. "Is this the best report you could produce?" "Why do you still work there?" "Aren't you dumping him?" But criticism can't be hidden with a question mark. No one is fooled by "Wouldn't you feel better if you practiced a few more times for tomorrow's presentation?" "Shouldn't someone your age be higher up in the company?" or "Tell me again exactly what you do for a living?"

Loaded questions can also make people look stupid, prove they are wrong, or highlight a weakness. "So what are you really saying?" "Why haven't you completed that project yet?" "Don't you know that punctuation goes within the quotation marks?" "Why don't you have the numbers?" "Why do you repeat yourself so much during meetings?"

No matter how you may try to disguise them, leading and loaded questions invariably cause trouble because they demonstrate that you aren't really concerned with what the other person thinks. These questions don't promote communication; they promote the questioner's agenda, reinforcing the counterproductive slide away from we-based to I-based communication.

Interrogating Questions

Interrogating questions make you sound like you're a police detective breathing down someone's neck. "How could you spend $200 taking that prospect to lunch? Don't you know how excessive that is? What were you thinking?" Questions designed explicitly to pin blame on someone will usually trigger negative responses.

Interrogating questions signal that the verdict is already in and that we're not genuinely searching for an alternative explanation or looking for dialogue; we've made up our minds and we want a guilty plea. Questions like this signal that we really don't want open communication, even as we ask for a response. This conversational bind is a core problem with many faulty questions that usually produces dissonance and distrust.

To avoid sounding like the stereotypical "bad cop" or aggressive trial lawyer, don't ask too many questions in a row, don't get too personal or too probing with your questions, and balance your inquiries with some sharing of your own in the conversation. Additionally, avoid putting your conversational partner in a dialogue-stifling defensive posture by eliminating phrases like *how could you* and *don't you know* from the beginning of your questions.

Identity Questions

Identity refers to a person's core beliefs and most deeply held feelings and sheds light on a foundational personal question: "Who am I?" People identify with their work, their religion, their family, their avocations, their nation, and other things that are meaningful to them. (We'll talk more about identity issues in Chapter 14.)

The rewards that come from asking someone about his core beliefs also come with a warning about the potential damage. Questions that respectfully give another person an opportunity to talk about something dear to them can draw people closer together. To a social worker: "I'm thinking of switching careers. Please tell me how you decided to become a social worker." To a Spaniard: "This is my first trip to Spain. Can you tell me a little about your country so I get a better feel for it?" To a Buddhist: "I don't know much about Buddhism. Could you give me an overview?"

But faulty questions that touch on identity topics can open up a great distance between people. To a social worker: "I'm thinking of switching careers and becoming a social worker. But how come social workers get paid so little?" To a Spaniard: "This is my first trip to Spain. Why do people here sleep during the day?" To a Buddhist: "I don't know much about Buddhism? Don't you find meditation boring? And why do you still eat hamburgers if you believe in reincarnation?"

What should you do if someone asks you a faulty question? The most important thing is to make sure that your response doesn't escalate the conversation. Ignore any obligation you feel to answer, and don't jump too quickly to assume the other person has a malicious intent. A question you perceive as faulty may only require clarification to get the conversation back on track. If you're still not sure about a question, delay your response and give the other person an opportunity to correct herself.

Questions are higher-order communication tools that people often offer into conversations with little or no forethought. This casual approach to questioning means that good people—including you and me—ask bad questions all the time.

A Question Is a Terrible Thing to Waste

Bad questions put distance between people. Good questions facilitate good communication, which strengthens relationships and improves our quality of life. That's why questions deserve more attention than they usually receive.

People need to perceive a meaningful purpose before they'll answer you without protective or evasive maneuvers. We see it all the time on police TV shows, but it's equally true in real life. When people don't feel safe, it's natural for them to offer "faux answers," to reply with something contrived, or to provide the bare minimum response.

Legitimate answers can't be coerced, so it's up to the person asking the question—in this case, you—to signal your good intentions. When you do, questions can work their magic as catalysts of meaningful exchange.

This doesn't mean that tough, important questions are off-limits. Good questions are essential in helping people make sense of challenging situations, performance failures, personality clashes, and business threats and opportunities.

And most people will answer questions about difficult subjects when they perceive a meaningful underlying intent. But if they think a question is designed to hang the blame or build a case against them, their responses will be much less helpful and much more reserved.

There are seven valuable tips to improve your questions:

1. **Clarify your intent.** The perception of a meaningful underlying intent is vital to effective questioning. If you sense uncertainty in your conversational partner, clear it up by saying something like "I'm trying to figure out how we might improve our future client pitches," "I'd like to know more about the way you work so our collaboration can be more effective," or "I want to learn how the Smith presentation went off track so we can try to win them back."

2. **Get and give permission.** Don't overlook the simple idea of asking permission: "May I ask you a question?" You can also tell the other person he doesn't have to answer: "Can I ask you some questions about the Smith presentation? You don't have to answer them if you don't want to." Giving people a sense of control in the conversation and a choice about answering often helps them feel like the conversational ground is safe for responding.

3. **Ask open questions whenever possible.** Open questions (and nudges, see the last tip we discuss) are designed to be answered in paragraphs, not in a few words.[3] This gives the other person freedom to respond and avoids unintentionally shutting off helpful information.

For example, asking "Did you feel like the Acme presentation went well?" is structured to produce a yes-or-no response. Even if the respondent tells you more, the question focuses attention on the success of the past presentation, when it's possible that what you really need to talk about is something the presenter heard the client say to a colleague or perhaps a funny feeling the presenter has about the client's new marketing director.

These things *might* come out in response to a closed question about the presentation, but the responder would have to make an effort to swim against the tide of the closed question. Remember, people are busy, so when we ask questions that can be answered in a few words—when we give them the ability to shortcut a more extended response—they'll often take it.

Here are some of the most versatile open questions:

> ➤ What do you think?
> ➤ How do you feel about this?
> ➤ What else should I know?
> ➤ What questions can I answer?

Additionally, you can readily construct open questions by using the phrases *how did, how was, please describe, please explain, please discuss,* and *please tell me more* (for example, "Please tell me more about your idea." "How did you feel about that?" "Please discuss the Gatorville account proposal." and "Please explain your conclusion in more detail.").[4]

4. **Be polite.** You'll notice that *please* occurs frequently in the examples above. This is pragmatic etiquette. Adding a *please* to your questions helps to signal your positive intent, which can reduce resistance and get the discussion started.

5. **Let people talk.** Let your good questions work their magic. Don't sabotage your questions by being afraid of silence. A pause following a good question usually signals contemplation, not consternation. If you jump in too quickly, you shortchange the process.

6. **Use closed questions prudently.** Closed questions can be answered in a handful of words and often start with words like *who, when, where, is,* or *do*: "Who can help us get this done?" "When is the project due?" "Where do I get more information?" "Is this the job you want?" and "Do you like your boss?" Closed questions are useful for simple informational queries ("When is the meeting?" "Is Sally still our HR contact?"), for limiting the range of potential responses, or for expediting a conversation.[5] But be very careful not to slip into the habit of closing off your questions when you are trying to establish dialogue and encourage conversational participation.

7. **Use nudges liberally.** Nudges are stand-alone phrases like *tell me more, I see,* and *go on,* which are often used following an open question to maintain the smooth flow of information.[6] Nudges are simple but effective ways to keep a line of inquiry active.

Learning to ask better questions will improve your relationships. You'll avoid some conflicts, and you'll insert less confusion and anxiety into your conversations. Better questioning skills will reduce resistance to your queries and help you establish more productive dialogue.

Good questions promote good communication, but effective questioning alone won't achieve our conversational goals. For that, we have to add some elbow grease and noodle juice. We have to prepare for conversations that matter.

8

IGNORE YOUR (TELLTALE) HEART

IT WANTS YOU TO TALK WITHOUT A PLAN

n a memorable passage from Lewis Carroll's *Alice's Adventures in Wonderland*, Alice asks the Cheshire cat what direction she should take in the woods. The cat asks Alice where she wants to go, and when Alice replies that she doesn't really care, the cat says, "Then it doesn't matter which way you go."

The cat put his paw on a lesson about communication: if we don't care how an interaction turns out, it doesn't matter how we approach it. But when conversations matter, it helps to have a destination in mind.

Casual conversations don't need an underlying goal or even a direction. Work—and life—wouldn't be much fun without the opportunity for friendly chitchat and informal banter. Jim in accounting shares your love of dogs, Sarah always has something nice to say, Bill knows the company history and folklore, and Jane never runs out of funny stories. Impromptu, casual conversations make our workplaces more enjoyable and our relationships more fun.

We don't need to prepare for these moments. All we need to do is safeguard enough of our time and attention to let them happen and to keep the exchange civilized so that a casual conversation doesn't escalate into a damaging one.

But many of our conversations are purposeful. Sometimes, you need to talk to Jim about next week's board meeting. You need to find out from Sarah why her report is late, again. You need to learn from Bill why a competitor keeps taking your leads or to discuss an employee's erratic behavior with Jane. These conversations are *strategic* because you are trying to accomplish something, and all strategic conversations require higher-order communication skills to accomplish your underlying objective.

Strategic conversations benefit from preparation, but it's hard to imagine something more anachronistic in the informal, always-on, I-need-an-answer-now digital age than *preparing* to communicate. Instead, we career through conversational intersections without considering where we're trying to go, leaving the Cheshire cat and his perceptive response as little more than a blurry fuzzball in our rearview mirror.

Most Conversations That Wander Are Lost

Andrea ran into some trouble at work. She'd missed a few deadlines and lost a client as a result. The financial impact hadn't hit her monthly revenue numbers yet, but she knew that when it did, Thomas, her boss, would want to talk to her. The conversation felt imminent, and the more Andrea contemplated it, the more agitated she became. The damage had already been done, she thought, and she just wanted to get past it.

So instead of waiting for Thomas to bring up the conversation, Andrea decided to be preemptive. She knocked on his office door and asked to talk. Still staring at his computer screen, he motioned for her to come in, and even before she sat down, Andrea was talking.

Her only "preparation" for the conversation had been listening to her own anxiety and wanting to share her side of the story. If she could talk to Thomas, she knew she could assure him that there was nothing to worry about.

Andrea started to describe the impact of losing the client and slipped in a few comments about how troublesome the company had been to work with. She was sure he'd see it her way. But within seconds, it was apparent that instead of winning Thomas to her side, her tangled and defensive words were thoroughly confusing him. He hadn't been thinking about the client before this, and now was trying to figure out exactly what the conversation was about.

That's funny, Andrea thought as Thomas's curious expression turned to a frown, *I pictured it going so much smoother.* As she tried to circle back to the missed deadlines and explain herself better, Andrea somehow managed to confuse even herself. Feeling increasingly desperate, she kept talking—even though it was talking that got her into trouble in the first place.

The conversation that Andrea started confidently ended in disheartening failure. Thomas didn't understand her side of the story, and after the conversation, the loss of the client—not a major account—loomed larger than it probably should have. As she walked back to her desk, knowing that she'd made things worse, Andrea knew that it was actually all her fault.

She should have paid more attention to the talking cat.

Fire, Ready, Aim Is Not a Strategy

Strategic conversations like Andrea's vary in how consequential they are and in whether they are expected or unexpected. All strategic conversations (including the unexpected ones, which we address later in the chapter) benefit from preparation.[1]

Unhelpfully, the more important a conversation feels, the less we want to delay it. We charge unprepared into important interactions, ignoring early warning signs that things aren't going well as we continue to pile on more counterproductive talking.

High-consequence conversations don't happen often. You may only have conversations like this a couple of times per month, but the relational stakes are serious each time. Examples of high-consequence conversations include:

➤ Communicating bad news at work or at home

➤ Asking for a raise or a new work assignment

➤ Seeking resolution of a longstanding dispute with a colleague

➤ Resolving a disagreement with an important client

➤ Initiating a conversation that leads to dissolution of a personal or professional relationship

➤ Seeking a consensus with siblings about how to care for an elderly parent

➤ Reaching out to a family member in a time of dire need

➤ Trying to reestablish a connection with a difficult family member

Most of us have less consequential, but still strategic, conversations almost daily. These low-consequence situations include:

➤ Convincing a colleague to attend a meeting in your place

➤ Asking your boss to extend a report deadline

➤ Persuading a coworker to edit a report one more time

➤ Convincing a spouse that a vacation in Hawaii is preferable to visiting the in-laws

➤ Coaxing a friend to take you to the airport

➤ Encouraging a relative to visit for the weekend

All strategic conversations—from low to high consequence—benefit from preparation.

Here's how to prepare for conversations that matter.

GAS Drives Strategy

There are three questions to consider when you prepare for an important conversation: What's your conversational *goal*? How will you *approach* your goal? And how will you *start* the conversation? Your goal directs your effort, focuses your attention, and helps you cut through a haze of distractions. Your *approach* helps you consider and select the appropriate tactics for goal attainment. And your *start* gets you off on the right foot. Together, they give you the easy-to-remember GAS preparation sequence.[2]

To illustrate how to use the GAS sequence, let's use an example from my consulting work, when a 30-year-old apartment manager was preparing for a conversation with a resident who had a history of verbally berating and insulting the manager and her staff.

Goal: *What's Your Conversational Goal?*

Your goal for any strategic conversation should be optimistic, but realistic, and stated simply. The goal is your orientation point throughout the conversation, the idea you keep at the front of your mind and where you can refocus the conversation if tangents, escalations, or other detours cause a drift.

The apartment manager decided that her goal was to get the resident to stop verbally abusing her and her staff. She also wanted to protect the underlying relationship, which was under strain because of his behavior, and she wanted to prevent further deterioration. She knew not to make the mistake of believing that things were so bad that they couldn't possibly get worse. Bad communication makes everything worse.

Whenever possible, resist the urge to have more than one goal for a single conversation. There's only so much a person can realistically accomplish in a single conversation, and multiple goals dilute everyone's focus. If you must have more than one goal, designate which is primary to help maintain your strategic focus.

When formulating your goal, consider what other, less favorable outcomes you could live with.

The apartment manager identified two possible alternatives if she couldn't meet her ultimate goal for the resident to stop verbally abusing her and her staff. The alternatives were:

➤ The resident could immediately break his lease and move out.

➤ The resident could keep his lease but would have to deal exclusively with a different manager in the future. (*Note:* This alternative assumed that the resident would be better behaved with a different manager. If this wasn't the case, the alternative wasn't viable.)

There are typically no more than two or three alternatives to any single goal, and there may not be any alternatives. If you continually find that there are no acceptable alternatives for your goal, it could be a signal that you aren't making a serious effort to develop other options. Also be alert for new options that may emerge during the conversation.

Remember, if you can't identify a conversational goal, you aren't having a strategic conversation. Important conversations that lack a clear focus are easily hijacked by potent emotions and unhelpful tangents. Without a clearly identifiable goal, not only are you likely to leave potential successes on the table, but you also increase the likelihood of compounding your problems as your conversation drifts from tangents to hazards.

Approach: *What Communication Approach Will Best Support Your Goal?*

The approach is the plan for *how* you will attain your goal; it represents the different ways to achieve your conversational purpose.

Many communication methods can help you achieve a goal, including using direct and indirect approaches; making analytical and emotional appeals; proposing choices; and reasoning. In a conversation, you might use a number of tactics together. For example, you might choose a direct approach, using facts and examples to buttress your point, and emphasizing the emotional angle of your case with a compelling story.

As she developed her approach plan, the manager considered several options:

➤ She could offer the resident a choice: he could modify his behavior and stay, or he could be allowed to break his lease and leave. People like choices, and tension can often be reduced when people feel like they selected the outcome.

➤ She could point out how the resident's behavior is making her and her staff feel, noting that while this is probably not what the resident intends, it is what's happening. This addresses the behavior but allows for some face-saving for the resident.

➤ She could briefly describe the most recent or most visible instance of the unwanted behavior, stating the ramifications of the behavior for her and her staff and making a direct request to stop the unwanted behavior.

The best conversational approach, however, is *identifying overlapping interests*. There will usually—somewhere—be an intersection between your interest and the other party's interest. As a quip widely attributed to Italian diplomat Daniele Vare states: "Diplomacy is the art of letting someone else have your way."

Smart communicators are conversational diplomats, lubricating the gears of human interaction to facilitate agreement, understanding, and harmony. Unfortunately, most people in conversations are more like plundering Vikings instead. They pillage their goals by responding to resistance with increasing force and intensity, which causes the other party's resistance to stiffen. Or they take an opposite approach and beg and grovel, behaviors that are equally ineffective because people tend to dislike and avoid perceived desperation.

Overlapping interests, on the other hand, encourage collaboration and offer better ways to achieve conversational goals. Ask yourself: *How does your proposal make the other person's life easier? How does your proposal solve a problem the other person is having? What's the benefit to the other party for supporting your idea?*

Don't mince words in showing your conversational partner the benefits—can you offer more time, money, freedom, and opportunity? Or less heartache, hassle, and paperwork? Clearly connect the benefits to the other person's life; it's even better when the other party gets in the spirit and points out shared interests you hadn't uncovered. For the apartment manager, there was an overlapping interest: the resident didn't want to move, and the apartment complex preferred to retain him as a tenant. Both parties would have had to take on additional costs if the resident left, which provided a shared incentive to resolve the issue.

In the small number of cases where there truly aren't any overlapping interests and where you want someone to take an action that won't benefit the person at all, don't make things up. It will quickly become obvious that you're trying to manipulate the interaction, and it will be self-defeating. When your proposal will bring the other party nothing but more work, extra hassles, and some new headaches, address the downsides directly but without fanfare. Be honest (but bland).

Start: *How Will You Start the Conversation?*

Good conversational openings put the other party at ease and prevent an immediate, negative reaction. Examples of possible openings include making a positive (but true) comment, giving a brief overview (to reduce conversational uncertainty), encouraging the other person's participation to develop a potential solution, or simply but gently stating the issue directly.

Openings matter because they can reduce the likelihood that the other person will reflexively resist your goal. Too many strategic conversations fail from the very first sentence because the other party assumes a defensive posture and prepares to resist before the issue is even addressed.

The apartment manager could have started the conversation by directly sharing her overlapping interest with the tenant that it would be better for both of them to work out an agreement that keeps the resident in his lease. Or she could have tried to draw the resident into participating in a solution by asking for his ideas about how to solve the issue (such a collaborative approach, although risky, can sometimes work).

In real life, when the apartment manager talked with the resident, she realized that he had no idea his words were causing such distress. After she gave him the space and time to say a few face-saving things ("I've been under a lot of pressure at work; I'm feeling stressed out and not entirely myself"), he apologized, and there were no additional problems with the resident for the remainder of his lease.

Success, Surrender, or Stalemate

It's critical to know how to start a conversation, but at some point you'll also need to know how to head for the exits. In strategic conversations, bring the interaction to a close when you have achieved your conversational goal or an alternative (success), run into entrenched resistance or clear rejection (surrender), or feel that you've gone as far as you can go in the current conversation (stalemate).

Let's return to the apartment example: the apartment manager planned to exit the conversation in success, surrender, or stalemate.

Exit in success. She would conclude and exit a successful conversation when:

➤ The resident expressed remorse and promised to change his behavior.

➤ The resident agreed to one of her two alternatives or came up with a third alternative during the conversation that was mutually acceptable.

Exit in surrender or stalemate. She would exit a failing conversation when:

➤ The conversation escalated to yelling, profanity, or insults (surrender).

➤ The conversation deteriorated to stonewalling or a shutdown of meaningful exchange (stalemate).

➤ She felt like she couldn't or shouldn't go any further in the current conversation (stalemate).

It's hard to forget anything that ends poorly, and conversations are no exception. Research shows that endings exert a disproportionate influence on our recollections, because our brains lean heavily on endings as markers for events in long-term memory.[3]

A good ending enables you to lock in your goal or an alternative in successful conversations, and it helps you get out of conversations in surrender or stalemate before too much damage is done to the underlying relationship. Watch for exit cues (*Sounds like we have agreed to . . .; Good talking with you; Let's pick this up later; See you next week; I think we've about covered it*), and finish strong to help the conversation's ending be the beginning of a positive memory.

Surprise

We can usually prepare for important conversations, because we can see them coming. It doesn't take a clairvoyant to anticipate a discussion about our unspectacular performance after a series of work errors or to foresee a talk with our spouse after saying something less than charitable to the in-laws.

But sometimes an important conversation will surprise you. You learn that you're being reassigned due to a restructuring. A coworker offers you important, but negative, feedback. A direct report presents a grievance you didn't anticipate. In these cases, the best way for you to respond is to treat the initial interaction as an information-gathering phase, isolate it from any subsequent discussion, and ask to return to the conversation later, when you've had time to plan.

If you can't delay an unexpected strategic conversation—like when your boss is bending your ear—you'll have to think on your feet. In these situations, the most important thing for you to do is to gather the relevant information without escalating matters.

There are three guidelines to remember when you're surprised by a serious conversation.

First, push your surprise off to the side and listen closely to gather as much information as you can. What's this person trying to tell you? What's the purpose of the conversation? Focus on understanding the key information and the big picture, and don't let your mind wander.

Second, don't feel an obligation to respond immediately. You can frequently ask for a conversational delay of minutes, hours, or days after you've learned the most important information. ("I appreciate your feedback. Can we continue the conversation after I've had some time to think about it?" or "This information is a bit surprising. May I have a few minutes [or hours or days] to get my thoughts together?") When possible, pause an unexpected strategic conversation after you've gathered the relevant information, even if the delay is only a few minutes long, and use the time to prepare for the remainder of the discussion. Pick the conversation back up once you've had time to absorb the information and formulate a strategy.

Third, stifle your urge to immediately change the conversation's trajectory. If the surprising news is negative, like performance feedback or a transfer you don't want, you'll only make things worse by trying to take control of the conversation. There is information asymmetry at play when you are surprised by a serious and negative conversation. Because most people hate delivering negative information, they have probably thought about the conversation a great deal. You'll be trying to influence a conversation on the fly with someone who has been thinking about the subject for much longer. Push for a conversational delay once you have extracted the relevant information and come back when you can both be on more equal footing.

Won't Get Fooled Again

Talking is something we do all the time, so it's easy to think that preparing to talk is a waste of time. *I talk to Jane almost every day,* we think, *so why should I take the time to consider what I want to say before I start to say it?* We usually don't think through our social media posts either, even though it's mass communication, because the audience is invisible. But put us in front of a roomful of people to deliver a speech or presentation, and we suddenly become ardent preparers.

Fear motivates us to prepare for public speaking, but comfort fools us into thinking we can launch into strategic interpersonal conversations without getting ready. We rush into the interpersonal conversations that can change the arc of a career or a relationship unprepared, trusting our instincts to give us immediate and correct answers to emotional and consequential situations, while we burn the midnight oil getting slides together for presentations that are forgotten before we're even halfway through our deck. The problem with our logic is that the crucial moments in our lives typically happen one-on-one, not in front of an audience.

The consequence of winging it through important conversations is brutally simple: vital conversations don't go our way as often as they should. But tendency doesn't have to be destiny. Prepare for conversations that matter.

If all the talk about preparation has you worried about where you're going to find the time, read on. We're about to free up a bunch of space on your calendar.

9

DON'T SOLVE PROBLEMS

YOU ARE MESSING AROUND WITH FAR TOO MANY ISSUES ALREADY

Growing up in Texas in the 1970s, I didn't know what inflation was, but I gathered from the adult conversations all around me that it wasn't good.

Decades later, fears of a '70s-style repeat (or worse) keep economic inflation in the news. But while we collectively worry about how much we may have to pay for a gallon of milk, we're largely overlooking a different threat: *communication inflation*.

Just as an inflated dollar loses its buying power, our dramatically increased rates of communication have cheapened our messages. We suffer from chronic transmission overload, pervasive distraction, and cascading communication problems as too many people weigh in on too many issues. As a result, it often takes more time and more energy to transmit even relatively straightforward messages. We need to regain the purchasing power of our words.

Five human tendencies make us susceptible to communication inflation:

1. **We love to talk.** The primordial human desire to connect fuels a great deal of our communication. Almost 2.5 billion people have social networking accounts, over 2.6 billion have instant message accounts, over 5 billion people—out of 7 billion globally—have cell phones, and an estimated 10 *trillion* e-mails are sent annually (and that doesn't include spam).[1] Humans love to communicate, and now we have convenient, powerful, and affordable ways to do so.

2. **We are action oriented.** Humans are doers. This is why it feels so good to hammer out an e-mail, fire off a text message, or reflexively respond to an instant message. Quick, cheap, and easy communication is an indulgence that makes us feel like we are accomplishing something. Unfortunately, those bursts of gratification fan the inflationary flames. The resulting glut of messages makes it difficult to isolate and act on conversations that can't wait. We scurry from nonissues to faux crises to contrived dilemmas, while more difficult situations stack up and become major problems.

3. **We instinctively pay attention to social messages.** People have been keeping an eye on the Joneses since those neighbors brought home their first pelt. We pay keen attention to social cues, scanning our environment for information that helps us understand what's going on and where we fit into the social structure. We collect and try to process an overwhelming amount of information. We don't want to miss anything that's happening in our immediate environment, even if much of it is of marginal value.

4. **We like solving problems.** We are the species that invented duct tape, superglue, and sticky notes. We like fixing things. Long before we used our opposable thumbs

to punch out smartphone messages, we were using them to pick up sticks and rocks to fashion tools and solve problems. This propensity remains with us today and explains why we often jump into issues that only tangentially relate to us. Put a problem in our inbox and we will instinctively try to solve it.

5. **We underestimate communication's ability to create problems.** We are also an optimistic, never-quit, sun-will-come-out-tomorrow, next-time-will-be-better people. And while our optimism has many upsides, it does create a quirk: we discount the number of problems that bad communication causes in our lives, while simultaneously exaggerating communication's problem-solving capabilities. The reality is that not all problems have a communication solution, and bad communication can cause more trouble than we can readily fix, even with an endless supply of duct tape and superglue.

Our smartphones and computers make it easier than ever to indulge our desires to jump into conversations. Take an action-oriented, problem-solving, social people who inherently love to talk and give them powerful communication devices, and the result is, in hindsight, entirely predictable: hypercommunication. With all of us empowered to chip in our two cents, it's no wonder that the result is inflationary. Our quick, cheap, and easy digital devices allow us to have far too many unnecessary conversations, engage in way too much unnecessary collaboration, and get our hands (and thumbs) on too many irrelevant issues.

The solution to communication inflation is simple: engage in fewer conversations. Avoid some conversations entirely and delay countless others. All we need is a method to separate conversations we should have immediately from all the others so we can stop trying to solve every issue that comes our way.

For a model, let's turn back the clock.

Napoleon Bonaparte's surgeon-in-chief, Dominique Jean Larrey, was a pioneer in emergency medical care and was one of the first battlefield surgeons in history. Among Larrey's many innovations were the so-called flying ambulances—horse-drawn carriages that could rapidly extract the wounded from the battlefield. Larrey also developed and advocated techniques for effective amputations, trading damaged limbs for the lives of innumerable Napoleonic soldiers.

But Larrey's primary contribution was something that is now common in medicine, but it was transformative at the time. Larrey is the father of *triage*—the allocation of emergency care, especially during times of calamity, to maximize overall survivability.[2] Prior to Larrey's system, there was no consistent way to evaluate and then treat patients most in need of care following a sudden influx of wounded. Wounded, but treatable, soldiers died waiting for care while medical staff worked with less critical—or sometimes less treatable—cases. Larrey developed a system elegant in its simplicity and powerful in its utility: evaluate each case as it arrives in order to allocate scarce resources for maximum effect.

Triage classification systems have evolved since Napoleon's era, but they are still, at the core, descendants of Larrey's simple and functional scheme.[3] When triage is used properly, doctors and patients benefit as time, energy, and resources help the greatest number of people.

Conversational Triage

Today we struggle with the lack of the same resources—time and energy—that Larrey did two centuries ago. Smart communicators, like smart doctors, have a good triage system to focus on the most pressing issues, while delaying or ignoring less important matters.

Effective conversational triage has never been more necessary, as the communication revolution's explosion of data, information, and connections brings us more issues to sort through than ever before. We can't afford to let the walking wounded push ahead of the gravely injured, and we don't have the resources to send hangnails in for surgery.

Applying the following three categories of conversational triage—Now, Delay, and Avoid—will help you free up that precious time and energy you need.

Now: Problems That Require an Immediate Conversation

Problems in the Now category require an immediate, solution-based conversation. Don't automatically assign too many issues to the Now category—this is the fundamental miscalculation that your triage system is trying to correct—or the resulting inflation will soak up your resources. If you're not sure if something is a Now issue, try delaying it and see what happens.

Examples of Now category problems can include:

➤ Problems that are part of a legitimate crisis or problems that have a valid, time-sensitive component[4]

➤ Problems you have reason to believe will get worse if not dealt with immediately

➤ Almost all problems brought to you by your boss, crucial employees, key stakeholders, or vital colleagues[5]

➤ Problems brought to you by people who seldom bring you problems

➤ Problems connected to the small number of areas you have identified as crucial to your professional success

➤ A problem you recently put in the Delay category that has returned

Any one of the parameters on the list is sufficient to require immediate handling; a problem that touches multiple parameters should galvanize your attention.

Delay: Problems Where Delaying the Conversation Makes Sense

Delay is your default category. Many issues don't need your active intervention, and you will probably be pleasantly surprised to find that delaying conversations, can, over time, encourage some problems to disappear completely or to resolve themselves without your participation.

Examples of Delay category problems include:

➤ Problems that you think will either go away or resolve themselves without your intervention (many issues that come to your attention probably go here)

➤ Problems that have resulted from conversational escalation and are now disconnected from root issues

➤ Problems that someone else (like peers or direct reports at work or family members at home) can and should solve without you

➤ Problems with no crucial time component, where a delay may result in better information, or problems that may become more clearly defined in the future

For all but obvious Now issues, make Delay your conversational default. Delay prevents premature action, buys time, and may allow solutions to emerge organically. A delayed issue that really belongs in the Now category will usually reappear quickly, at which point you can (and probably should) address it.

It's best to delay without fanfare; just avoid or otherwise put off the conversation. If the other person knows that you are delaying and it bothers him, provide a legitimate external excuse if you have one ("I'm way behind on my e-mails from being out of town" or "I'm late for a meeting") or offer another time to talk. If he won't be delayed, let him talk without adding anything substantive. Don't indicate that you think a delayed conversation is unimportant or an escalation could make it important for the wrong reason.

Avoid: Problems That Are Too Hard and Too Volatile to Handle

Some issues reflect highly emotional, incredibly complicated, and other volatile feelings that reside deep inside another person. While these kinds of problems occasionally crop up at work, they don't have readily identifiable solutions—and may have no solution at all—so tackling them with a fix-it mentality can cause serious damage.

There are some emotional and sensitive issues that people have to wrestle with alone or with a professional counselor, clinician, or advisor. Provide support and encouragement when you sense that people need it, but in general, steer clear of Avoid issues unless there is absolutely no way around them and the issues are impairing the accomplishment of critical work.

Examples of Avoid category problems can include:

➤ Problems stemming from a traumatic personal experience, like an accident or an incident

➤ Pivotal childhood experiences that are buried under layers of time and imperfect, confusing memories

➤ Issues of a deeply personal nature that are often extremely complicated and that frequently generate confusion and conflicting emotions when discussed

➤ Complicated intrafamily conflicts that span multiple generations

There are a very small number of highly sensitive issues in the Avoid category, so placing more than a handful of issues in this category is almost certainly an indication that you're avoiding problems that you should handle.

Most legitimate Avoid category issues are personal in nature and not routinely discussed at work. You are most likely to uncover Avoid problems as you get to know people in depth, with direct reports, or when you are involved in close collaboration. People you barely know or seldom work with will try hard to keep their Avoid issues to themselves. Should you stumble into an Avoid category problem, people will usually alert you with comments like "I'm trying to put that behind me," "I'd rather not talk about it," or "Let's not go there." Take them at their words.

Deeply personal and emotional issues like the examples on the previous list frequently defy understanding and don't readily lend themselves to solutions. Such problems are usually in a person's too-hard box for good reasons, so switch topics or tactfully end the conversation when an Avoid issue comes up. If the other person feels like talking—and if you want to listen—lend him your ears, but don't actively probe for more information. Let your conversational partner decide how much he's comfortable disclosing. You can always switch topics or exit if you feel like the conversation is pushing past the appropriate boundaries of your underlying relationship.

When an Avoid problem is hindering essential work, look for a way to temporarily or permanently address the issue and, when possible, encourage the other person to seek professional help for the issue if you think your relationship can support your being this direct. (For subordinates, you can be this direct. Point them to professional resources if an Avoid issue is impairing essential work tasks.)

For example, if a colleague is freezing up in front of a forceful client because the aggressive behavior reminds your coworker of an abusive parent, you can handle the interactions with the client for the next few months (temporary solution), you can interact with the client exclusively in the future (permanent solution), or you can encourage your colleague to seek professional help (possibly a permanent solution). If a subordinate is unproductive for hours at a time due to a traumatic accident or incident, you might reassign some of her key tasks while helping her access the proper resources to work through the issue. Hopefully, the professional help will lead to a positive permanent solution.

Today, billions of people in our human tribe—the tribe that loves to solve problems, take action, and keep up with the Smiths and Hus—are sending trillions of messages. It's time to take a page from Dominique Jean Larrey's playbook and stop trying to engage in all the conversations that come our way.[6] It's time to implement a functional conversational triage system. Once our triage system is in place, we can protect the discussions we do have from minor hazards by using conversational shock absorbers.

10

BLOW
THINGS OFF

PROTECT WHAT MATTERS BY
LETTING GO OF WHAT DOESN'T

y niece, Iris, and her best friend, Nina, walk together to kindergarten each morning. The walk is only a few blocks, and they talk the entire way. Their conversations are full of laughter and singing, but my sister tells me that squabbling, misunderstandings, and tears are also not uncommon.

Even in kindergarten, when our lives and our relationships are simpler, all kinds of familiar hazards can happen when we communicate. We lose our train of thought and botch our message. We talk over the other person. We misinterpret a comment, make an incorrect assumption, take words out of context, say something that's supposed to be funny but isn't, render an awkward comment, say something half-baked and confusing, or sometimes simply don't understand what the other person is saying. Communication can bring us some of our most enjoyable moments, but it is fundamentally—and irreparably—imperfect.

The hazards have multiplied with the digital revolution, as we communicate with more people, in more ways, than ever before. Just like quadrupling the length of your daily commute would result in encountering more road hazards, more communication results in more imperfect (and often irritating) communication issues.

Furthermore, the increase of asynchronous communication in the digital age creates additional trouble. When we decrease our nonverbal conversational cues like tone of voice, body positioning, and gesturing (signals that are all absent in asynchronous communication), we increase the potential for misunderstandings and confusion. And we also receive less timely feedback about the effectiveness of our communication due to the lag between our message and a response.

Without protective measures, conversational hazards can easily escalate into damaging relational incidents. We may criticize someone for being unprepared when a part of his presentation just came out wrong. We might misconstrue an awkward conversation as a harbinger of trouble and overcompensate during the next interaction. We sometimes misinterpret a confusing e-mail and fire off a harsh response.

Since we can't completely eliminate communication hazards no matter how hard we try, we need to create a buffer—what we'll call relational shock absorbers—to dampen the impact of inevitable hazards and smooth out some of the rough spots in everyday communication. Without shock absorbers, we are in for a long and teeth-rattling ride on the communication superhighway.

Conversational Shock Absorbers

There are four shock-absorbing communication behaviors that smooth out the majority of common interpersonal hazards.

1. Let Go

Have you ever been able to work with someone when it seemed no one else could? Or talk to a relative who drives everyone else in your family crazy? Do you have close friends at work or at home who seriously irritate other people, but not you? If so, this success is almost certainly because you can ignore behaviors that other people can't. You allow a do-over where other people insist on keeping score. That's letting go, and it's also the difference between my niece's walks to school that end in laughter and the ones that end in tears.

When we let go of all but the most serious transgressions that touch us, we preempt damaging escalations and provide a chance for people to self-correct. You shouldn't let serious breaches go, but most interpersonal hazards aren't major. Letting go is communication's equivalent of golf's Mulligan—an errant stroke that doesn't count against a golfer's score. If you let people take a Mulligan when they need one, they'll probably return the favor. In light of communication's imperfectability (and human fallibility), you'll both find that interpersonal do-overs come in handy.

And don't worry that extending Mulligans will perpetuate bad behavior. In the unlikely event that someone seems to take advantage of your willingness to overlook the occasional mistake, you can always stop ignoring the behavior or have a direct conversation about the issue.

Although asynchronous communication makes conversational hazards more likely because of the lack of cues and delayed feedback, the good news is that it's often easier to let go of asynchronous communication hazards. You can use the lag inherent in asynchronous communication between receiving a message and responding to avoid a knee-jerk reaction and to reply more thoughtfully. And when people can't see you receiving a message, there is always a little uncertainty about whether it went through or whether you've seen it yet, which makes it easier to ignore. So whenever possible, let asynchronous conversational hazards die on the digital vine—take an e-Mulligan—by ignoring the mildly irritating e-mail, text message, or social media post.

You can also proactively use digital devices to insert shock-absorbing space between you and your conversational partner when it might be beneficial. A friend of mine, who acknowledges he has a temper, has an agreement with his wife to only communicate via text message when he's upset. This keeps a line of communication open between them, but it gives him an asynchronous channel to constrain and delay his responses, the hope being to prevent him from saying something he'll regret later. When he's cooled off enough, they can continue their discussion face-to-face or by phone.

This example also provides a good opportunity to repeat an important point: our new communication devices don't degrade our interactions; we do. It's entirely possible—indeed, it's the great promise of the digital communication revolution—to use digital devices in ways that improve our communication and strengthen (or prevent damage to) our most important relationships. Our devices are remarkable communication tools. How we use our tools is in our hands.

2. Assume Good Intentions

A few years ago, my wife and I were at a gas station, and I used my fingers to count up how much a few items would cost. The clerk, trying to be funny, fumbled a joke and essentially implied that I was stupid. I laughed along with him. When we got outside, my wife wanted to know why I was laughing with someone who had insulted me.

The clerk, I replied, didn't *intend* to insult me. He tried to be funny, but he failed because humor is an incredibly difficult communication behavior to pull off. By laughing, I responded to the *intended* joke, not the *unintentional* insult. When I walked out of the store laughing, the clerk remained inside with a smile on his face.

That's how a shock absorber works, smoothing the negative potential in an encounter and eliminating damage before it has a chance to occur. On the other hand, being hypervigilant and ready to correct every mistake—the opposite of assuming good intentions—will mentally exhaust you, degrade your conversations, and keep you busy reacting to communication's innumerable hazards. If you go looking for errors, imperfect communication will deliver, and meaningful communication will become ever more elusive.

We're too quick to blame people for conversational errors even when there are often situational factors—like routine conversational hazards—that reduce or eliminate their culpability. This bias to discount situational explanations is so prevalent that it's known to social scientists as the *fundamental attribution error*.[1] Assuming good intentions is an effective countermeasure against the fundamental attribution error. Besides, if another person's intentions are less than honorable, you'll have plenty of opportunities to figure that out.

3. Give and Accept Apologies Quickly

In 2006, Academy Award–winning actor Mel Gibson was driving drunk when a deputy from the Los Angeles Sheriff's Department pulled him over. Instead of trying to contain the damage, Gibson converted a bad situation into a horrendous one by letting loose with a string of eye-watering, reputation-shattering, anti-Semitic remarks and profanities that rapidly surged around the Internet.

Gibson suffered a profound blow to his reputation; even devoted fans were appalled by his fiery remarks. He eventually apologized, but not before irrevocable damage was done to his reputation and his career. The court of public opinion would most likely have forgiven Mel Gibson's DUI charge—he certainly wouldn't be the first celebrity with a police record—but his inflammatory words created a hole that was just too deep.

Some words are so explosive that apologies won't make a significant difference in reducing the harm. *But these are not the kind of errors most people make.* Spectacular blow-ups get the press, but most errors are accidental, only mildly offensive, and eminently recoverable.

There's often a brief period of time just after an error—what we call a period of conversational amnesty—when all but the most serious transgressions are usually easily forgiven. If you've said something inappropriate or insensitive, a quick apology can reduce the harm.[2]

Mel Gibson's mistake—escalating the transgression phase instead of stopping it—cost him dearly, and he's not alone. Research suggests that after making an initial mistake, people will often continue digging a hole instead of putting down the shovel. Even though it's self-defeating behavior, reversing course feels inconsistent.[3]

If you find yourself with ill-chosen words hanging in the air and a shovel in your hand, stop digging deeper and start patching the hole. Apologize as soon as you realize you need to do so—ideally during the shock-absorbing amnesty period.

There are four elements to apologies: (1) taking responsibility, (2) expressing remorse, (3) promising not to repeat the offense, and (4) offering to redress the wrong.[4] You can remember them as the four Rs:

Responsibility

Remorse

(won't) **R**epeat

Redress

Studies of apology effectiveness indicate that you only need to use one or two of the four Rs.[5] So consider some variant of

"I'm sorry, this mistake is my fault." That sentence alone covers two Rs—remorse and responsibility—making it a very good way to apologize.

4. Implement a 60-Second Rule

Look around the next time you're at a wedding reception, and you'll probably see that the dancers are having more fun than the wallflowers. Indeed, there's evidence to suggest that dancing in groups is a reliable way to boost happiness.[6]

Even though I know this is true, I often have to talk myself onto the dance floor. When I dance, I spend a disproportionate share of time worrying that I'm making a fool of myself. My wife assures me that no one cares how I look. Besides, she points out, it's impossible to look elegant when moving to "Who Let the Dogs Out," a song that, for some reason, is a favorite at family weddings.

The awkwardness I feel on the dance floor is similar to the awkwardness that we sometimes encounter in conversations. We know there's a rhythm, but we can't seem to find it. What keeps people glued to their chairs at wedding receptions, and what makes people avoid conversations, is the perception that we're just not moving to the right beat.

Conversational hazards—a misunderstanding, a joke that fails, a pause that feels too long—often start a negative cycle by introducing that feeling of awkwardness, which in turn triggers distracting thoughts (*Why aren't they laughing? Why does this conversation feel so jerky? Ugh, I'm so terrible at small talk . . . I'll never get this job/land this client/get this date*), which invariably lead to more conversational mistakes and more awkwardness. At some point, the situation becomes unbearable, and someone ejects from the interaction, nerve-racked and embarrassed.

As I get older, I'm ignoring my inner dance critic and learning a few moves instead. I usually find a rhythm after a minute or so, and then I can relax and enjoy myself. The same solution applies to your communication; you can smooth your conversational moves with the shock absorbers we've already discussed, topped off with the *60-second rule*.

Hazards can happen throughout conversations, but they're especially prevalent at the beginning, when everyone is trying to find a rhythm. The 60-second rule requires that for the first minute of any interaction, you ignore all but the most serious or offensive transgressions as two people try to find a conversational rhythm. During a one-minute grace period, you choose to forgive and not draw attention to any silly or ham-handed remark that the person says. You also go easy on yourself.

The 60-second rule is liberating because it prevents many types of interactions from ever escalating and causing damage. So much of our communication comes in quick bursts from passing encounters, text messages, e-mails, or social media postings that the 60-second rule shock absorber will apply to large swaths of our day-to-day life. Talking to a sales clerk or a customer-service agent, asking a colleague a quick question, or engaging in a brief exchange with a stranger are almost always covered in their entirety by the 60-second rule. This means that you don't ever need to worry about an escalation when you leave the house to run an errand, walk to the water cooler, or pick up a to-go order.

Shockingly Good

In addition to reducing the chance of conversational escalation and relational damage, shock absorbers provide two other important benefits: they protect your goodwill account, and they facilitate positive reciprocal behaviors.

Your Goodwill Account

As you get to know people, you accumulate psychological credits (or debits) according to how someone perceives your words and deeds. Generally, when you say or do good things, you get credits, and when you say or do bad things, you draw down some of the credits. The result creates a goodwill account balance for each of your relationships, which rises and falls over time.

A positive goodwill balance has a major influence on how someone perceives you. When you have a goodwill surplus, the other person is more likely to give you the benefit of the doubt when things go wrong and full credit when things go right. He gives you a break when you need it, and he knows that you earned your successes. It's like an interpersonal heaven. But when you are in deficit, it's nothing but pitchforks. Your successes are discounted, and your failures are magnified. When things go wrong, it's your fault. When you succeed, it's because you got lucky. A goodwill account deficit is relational purgatory.

Naturally, we want to stay in interpersonal heaven (maintaining a positive goodwill balance) and keep out of interpersonal purgatory (avoiding a goodwill account deficit) so our successes and failures are seen in the best possible context. But we also want to maintain a positive balance, because every now and then we really mess up and cause a major jolt in a relationship.

You might lose an important client because you miss a delivery date. You might deeply upset your boss or a family member by crossing a personal boundary. Your big project might flop, to great embarrassment and cost. When big disruptions like this happen, you need a substantial goodwill surplus to draw on. Shock absorbers protect your vital store of relational goodwill by reducing or eliminating withdrawals from your account for common interpersonal hazards.

Applying shock absorbers to the multitude of smaller jolts and hazards that come up day to day means that when that larger shock comes along, your goodwill bank account will be in the best position to handle the large withdrawal. There's no guarantee that a positive goodwill balance will prevent relational dissolution after major shocks, but having plenty of goodwill in the bank increases the likelihood that you'll recover.

Finally, although many ideas in this book suggest that *not* saying something is often the smart communication move, your positive goodwill account gives you the opportunity—the obligation perhaps—to tackle sensitive issues when necessary. For example, you might need to spend a little of your goodwill reserve to initiate a discussion with a colleague whose behavior has changed so dramatically that you're concerned for her well-being. You might have a frank discussion with a good friend who's making an obvious mistake. You might raise an ethical objection to something your boss is doing.

These are all high-risk conversations that you'll probably only have a few times *in your entire life*. Pragmatically, you can only intervene so many times before people start dreading your presence, and that's not a good long-term career or relational strategy.

In high-risk conversations, by definition, the odds are against you. Your colleague will probably be depressed but not suicidal. Your friend will probably marry his fiancée no matter what you say. And your boss will, to say the least, probably not appreciate your intervention. But sometimes you may decide to take major risks against terrible odds, because you feel that the alternative—inaction—is unacceptable.

The point is that communication is *for something*. One reason to build positive goodwill balances is so we can go out on a limb for really important things and not worry that we are going to ruin a relationship. A healthy goodwill account gives you the ability—and the confidence—to take risks against the odds when it matters.

Protect, but don't hoard, your positive goodwill balance. You'll know when you need to use it.

Cascade of Reciprocity

A second benefit of shock absorbers is that they encourage a cascade of helpful relationship behaviors by activating reciprocity. Good behavior begets good and bad begets bad. Your shock-absorbing behaviors—*letting go, assuming good intentions, apologizing quickly,* and *adhering to the 60-second rule*—are likely to stimulate the same protective behaviors from your conversational partners, amplifying the cushioning ability and resilience in your relationships.

Shock absorbers reduce the potential for interpersonal harm and allow our most important relationships to thrive in spite of the minor jolts and irritating transgressions that are normal by-products of communication. They give us the confidence to get out on the conversational dance floor and enjoy the kinds of enriching, exhilarating, and meaningful connections that communication can provide.

Even with a good set of shock absorbers, communicating with a small number of difficult people is still a jolting experience. Don't worry, though; we have a strategy just for them. It's quitting time.

11

LET DIFFICULT
PEOPLE WIN

STOP TRYING TO IMPOSE YOUR
WILL ON TOUGH COMMUNICATORS

R ichard "Tuff" Hedeman earned his nickname. He was a
three-time world champion bull rider and one of the few
people ever to successfully ride the powerful and notorious
bull named Bodacious.[1]

Bodacious possessed an uncommon combination of power and
unpredictability, and had a nasty habit of contorting in ways that
other bulls wouldn't or couldn't. And as Tuff Hedeman learned,
Bodacious had a few other tricks up his hoof to shake off cowboys
who didn't have the sense to let go after the first few seconds.

Hedeman first successfully rode Bodacious in 1993, staying on
for the required eight seconds—an eternity on the back of Bodacious. Two years later, Hedeman drew Bodacious again at the
professional bull-riding finals in Las Vegas. Shortly after leaving the
chute, the bull lurched dramatically, whipping Hedeman backward
and forward like a rag doll. Then Bodacious jerked backward at full

speed, violently head-butting Hedeman and breaking his cheek-bones into 11 pieces.[2]

In a television interview, Hedeman described the surgery and its aftermath with characteristic understatement: "It took about six and a half hours of reconstructive surgery and six titanium plates, and I can't smell or taste anything, but I guess that comes in handy when there aren't any good restaurants around."[3]

Two months after the accident, with his face reconstructed, Tuff Hedeman drew Bodacious for the third time at the national rodeo finals. There was anticipation and some tension in the arena because Hedeman never backed down from a challenge—something that made him a fan favorite. But as the chute opened, before the bucking even began, Hedeman jumped off Bodacious and forfeited his turn.[4] He quit before Bodacious started.

As Hedeman tipped his hat to the bull, the crowd responded to his decision with an ovation. Not long after, Bodacious—although still in his prime—was retired. The bull was simply too dangerous for anyone to ride.

Ride a Bull, Meet a Nurse

Communicating with some people is a lot like climbing on the back of Bodacious—the situation is impossible to control, and no matter how hard you try, you still may end up in the dirt.

People are difficult in a number of ways. Jane talks too much. Jim is incredibly stubborn. Uncle Billy loves to argue. Your client is moody. The table on the next page provides a menu of different types.

Whether they're controlling, critical, or just cranky, the behaviors that make someone a difficult person present formidable barriers to productive and meaningful communication. Difficult people make we-based interpersonal communication extremely elusive, and sometimes downright impossible.

Common types of difficult people			
Argumentative	Talkative	Controlling	Sensitive
Stubborn	Quiet	Anxious	Passive-aggressive
Critical	Moody	Emotional	Attention-seeking
Cranky	Indecisive	Unmotivated	Confrontational

Difficult people also share a talent for provoking frustration, which activates the Neanderthal instincts inside us. When a particularly difficult colleague opens his mouth, part of your brain starts urging you to be assertive: *C'mon, Geoff, don't just stand there and let Jim get the best of you. Get in there and show him that he can't treat you like that.*

So we leap into confrontations with the very people we are least likely to influence. We wrestle with Jane to get a word in edgewise. We struggle to change Jim's mind. We fire a barrage of points and counterpoints into Uncle Billy's arguments. We try to offset our client's mood swings.

Alas, like many of the Neanderthal's prescriptions, treating difficult people like a challenge to overcome or a difficult conversation as a game to win doesn't work in the modern world. The Neanderthal approach makes a serious error when it encourages you to personalize a difficult person's behavior (*Look at how he's treating me; he can't do that to me*), because with difficult people it's not personal at all. Uncle Billy argues with *everybody*. Your client in Wichita Falls is moody with *everyone*. Jane will talk *anyone's* ear off. Jim is stubborn with *everyone*.

It's not you; it's them. You won't see that sentence anywhere else in this book, because we are at least partially responsible for virtually all of our communication problems. But difficult people are the exception.

The good news is that there aren't many truly difficult people in the world (even though they seem to be surrounding you on some days). Take a good, clear look at the people who push your buttons. If they're only difficult with you, that's a relationship problem, not a difficult-person problem. And if a person is only difficult occasionally, that's just a regular person having a bad day. When someone is only difficult with you (a relationship problem), figure out how you are contributing to the problem—which you almost certainly are—and adjust your own behavior first. If that doesn't improve the relationship, initiate a conversation to find out what will.

Although most people aren't chronically difficult, even one difficult person in a key role—a boss, a key client, or a close family member—can cause major frustration. But Neanderthal-induced strategies don't work well with difficult people. To communicate more effectively with such types, we need to take a page from Tuff Hedeman's Bodacious playbook.

We need to quit.

Difficult people don't change. At the end of a conversation, the difficult person remains the same, but often we are in a weaker position. Difficult communication is frustrating—and occasionally exhausting—communication. Frustration acts like a multiplier, amplifying our responses, increasing the escalation, and magnifying the relational damage. Whatever happens, we lose. The situation is rigged against us.

Quitting is not as outrageous as it sounds. You've probably already configured your life to reduce your exposure to as many difficult people as you can: coworkers you can avoid, old friends you can ignore, and clients you can do without. So keep up the good work.

The difficult people who will remain in your life are those you either *have to* or *want to* communicate with, like bosses, important clients, essential colleagues, and close family members. These people stay in your network, but this short list is manageable because, again, most people are not chronically difficult—and because you're going to quit trying to force your will on those who are.

Only a commitment to let go of our desire to "win" by imposing our will on the other person can realistically and consistently improve our communication with difficult communicators. Difficult people won't be controlled. It's time to quit.

The Zen of Quitting

Few players in NBA history were more difficult to handle than Dennis "the Menace" Rodman. Covered with tattoos and piercings and prone to kaleidoscopic hair dyeing, Rodman was difficult on and off the court. He was also one of the league's leading rebounders, making him an on-court asset despite his eccentric behavior. Many people—coaches, teammates, and NBA executives—admired Rodman's talents, but few people knew how to channel his skills.[5]

In his autobiography *Bad as I Wanna Be*, Rodman recalls how he quickly came to appreciate then–Chicago Bulls coach Phil Jackson:

> *When I looked over there during that first exhibition game and saw him laughing as the ref was slapping a T [technical foul] on me . . . I couldn't believe it. I wasn't expecting that. I wasn't ready for that. Somebody understands? **A coach who understands?** One thought came to my mind: **Finally.**[6]* [Emphasis in original]

Jackson—a 6' 8" former basketball player and a record-setting coach of professional basketball championship teams—had a nickname of his own, "Zen Master," for his legendary coaching style that incorporated Eastern, Western, Native American, and New Age spiritual practices with a serene sideline persona.[7]

Jackson was famous for not trying to overtly impose his will on players and for believing that his leadership was working when he was "invisible" and things were happening in the moment.[8] His ability to relinquish control and find ways to work with difficult players enabled him to deal with larger-than-life personalities like Rodman, Michael Jordan, Shaquille O'Neal, and Kobe Bryant—men who could twist other coaches into knots.

You might say that the most successful coach in professional basketball history was a quitter of sorts, just as you and I should be with difficult communicators.

Instructions for Quitters

You can't avoid difficult people all the time. Five suggestions will help you quit intelligently when you need to interact with the difficult—but important—people in your life:

1. **Let go.** Let difficult people be difficult. How people act is just a *tactic*, while what you want to achieve is a *strategy*. Let them have their tactics. Stay focused on your strategy.

2. **Aim low.** Scale back your conversational goals and accept the likelihood of failure that accompanies conversations with difficult people. Don't expect we-based interpersonal communication to emerge easily, if at all, in the conversation. Have modest expectations when you are dealing with difficult communicators.

3. **Avoid tangents.** *Goal, goal, goal*—stay focused on your (modest) conversational goal. Difficult people make frustrating conversational partners, and where frustration lurks, relational danger is never far away. Don't open or support extra lines of conversation when dealing with a difficult person; diversions will just increase the amount of time that you're exposed to a challenging interaction and will dilute your focus.

4. **Go private.** Have conversations with difficult people one-on-one whenever possible. Adding others to a difficult conversation only increases the uncertainty, adds complexity, opens the door for the difficult person to display more unhelpful behaviors (like showing off for another person), and raises the risk that the difficult person's behavior will contaminate the group.

5. **Get out.** Exit a conversation with a difficult person as soon as your goal has been fully or partially attained or when the conversation reaches a stalemate. If a difficult person initiates a conversation, be alert to contain the conversation and make an exit if the discussion becomes problematic.

Dealing with Four Common Types of Difficult People

There are four common types of difficult people—argumentative, stubborn, controlling, and quiet—who merit additional discussion.[9] Combine these suggestions with the five ideas we discussed earlier—*let go, aim low, avoid tangents, go private,* and *get out*—to improve your interactions with these difficult people.

Argumentative People

Some conversationalists put the devil in devil's advocate. They argue for any reason, they are relentless in pounding home their points, and they aren't above changing their position on the fly just to keep the argument going. Let these serial arguers have their say, because any attempts to squelch their arguments are likely to backfire. People like this will probably even argue with you about why you're trying to silence them.

It's helpful to track the serial arguer's habits and determine if he might be less combative at certain times of the day or through certain communication modes, like on the phone or face-to-face. If your argumentative boss is more agreeable right after lunch when he's not hungry, or by e-mail where he feels less pressure to respond immediately, schedule your strategic conversations accordingly.

Stubborn People

Stubborn people cause more frustrations than any other type of difficult person, because no matter what you do, they just don't budge much from their positions. Assign your lowest conversational expectations to these people. Set very modest goals for a conversation, like getting a stubborn person just to listen to you or securing the scantest of agreements. You might be able to build on small successes over time.

In order to moderate a stubborn person's reflexive and negative responses, it's sometimes helpful to ask for permission to bring up an issue. Tell the stubborn person that you aren't looking to change her mind, but you simply want to express yourself. Concisely state your position. If the other person listens, that's progress. You can't move stubborn people too far, too fast, if you can even move them at all.

Controlling People

Some people seize control of a conversation and don't let anyone else meaningfully impact its topics or trajectory. People control conversations for one of three primary reasons. In the first case, one person—like a boss, teacher, or parent—has formal authority and wields it to steer the conversation. In the second case, time constraints or a sense of urgency is driving the controlling behavior. And in the third case, the controller is worried about what might happen, and where the discussion might lead, if he doesn't direct the conversation.

When someone tries to control the conversation, your strategy should usually be simple: let the person do it. As long as your conversational goal (if you have one) isn't getting completely stifled, it's probably fine to let the other person lead the discussion.

But if the controlling behavior prevents you from reasonably addressing your conversational goal, you have a few options. You can tell the person that you have something to say. You can ask to switch topics. You can use questions and statements to insert your objective into the conversation ("Can I say something here?" "I have something to add to that." "I'd like to make a comment"). And if the controlling behavior is causing serious—not just irritating— relational problems, you can prepare for a conversation to directly address the behavior.

Quiet People

While some difficult people talk too much, others don't talk much at all; or if they do talk, they seldom share anything meaningful. If you have a key relationship with a quiet or reserved person and the lack of communication is causing problems, find a way to realistically increase her engagement in the conversations you need to have. Don't be afraid to thoughtfully talk about the communication that you feel is missing from your relationship with a quiet person, but be realistic about the probable outcomes.

A quiet person is not likely to suddenly open up about every issue. Think carefully about what you really need and prepare one or two specific and modest requests (such as to your boss: "Could we talk once a month about how I'm doing?" or "Could we talk once a quarter about my key projects?" And to your significant other: "Could we talk about the day ahead before we go to sleep each night?" or "I'd like it if you would share your concerns with me more often").

As we know all too well, difficult communicators make for frustrating interactions where we–based interpersonal communication is rare and our Neanderthal instincts are agitated. It never ends favorably when the Neanderthal climbs on top of Bodacious the bull.

Take a lesson from a cowboy named Tuff and a coach called the Zen Master instead. If you're willing to quit imposing your will on difficult people, your interactions with them will be less prone to damaging escalation.

Next, I need to ask you to do something even harder.

12

RESPOND WITH WEAKNESS

BRING A STICK TO A KNIFE FIGHT

My first course on my first day of college was boxing—a mandatory class at West Point. I vividly recall racing from that class to the showers and then to my chemistry class, my hair sometimes frozen in the cold New York air as winter set in.

I also remember that none of us really wanted to get hurt, so we pulled (faked) far more punches than we actually threw in that class. Most of us did, that is, but not Harry Haymaker, a mild-mannered classmate outside the ring and a terror inside it.[1]

We were all friends with Harry. But once the bell sounded, to the delight of our muscle-bound instructors, Harry would charge forward with both arms swinging. He had neither superior skill (it would be hard to call what he did "boxing") nor overwhelming strength. But he did have wild-eyed zeal. His advantage was that if he ever landed a lucky punch, you were going down.

Our faux fighting didn't entertain our instructors, who yelled at us to hit harder and knock somebody out.[2] They used Harry as punishment, making threats like "If you two don't quit dancing around like best friends, I'll make you box Harry."

It wasn't until our final boxing exams of four 3-minute rounds—a marathon compared with our previous sparring—that the limits of Harry's technique became painfully clear. He couldn't sustain his ferocious routine, and when he ran out of gas he got pummeled. No one pulled punches with Harry because he had hit us unnecessarily—and repeatedly—before.

Like Harry, we all too often use more interpersonal force than we need to accomplish our objectives. We yell when a measured response would work better, send a blistering e-mail when a more restrained reply would suffice, or issue an ultimatum when a firm but gentle statement of convictions would do. Excessive force is a club-first, think-later Neanderthal response, and it often boomerangs painfully back at us.

Conflicts that start or escalate with excessive force and intensity frequently cause a destructive cycle—attack, retaliation, escalated attack, and escalated retaliation—as each conversational turn adds new relational harm. According to researchers, verbal attacks and sharp criticism can cause damaging stress.[3] What started out as a conversation about how incoming mail should be processed, for example, may escalate into a series of demeaning comments about the value of one person's job over another and end with someone in the bathroom in tears.

I have a friend, Jason, who is a tenured professor and a respected scholar. Jason had a bruising encounter with his department chair, Steve, a few years ago when he learned that a new hire received a higher starting salary than he had received when he joined the department. My friend admits that he started the conversation off poorly by insinuating that Steve was unintelligent—a big putdown in academia—for approving the hire. Steve retaliated by pointing out all the reasons why the new hire was a superior scholar to Jason, which was also a major jab. The conversation got worse from there.

Weeks later, Jason and Steve eventually apologized to each other, but the damage was done. Although other influential professors expressed their support, Jason moved to another university the following year. Now, when Jason and his former department chair meet at academic conferences, they don't even speak. A multiyear relationship was dismantled in one encounter. Sadly, it happens all the time because of the asymmetry of communication.

John Gottman, a leading authority on relational conflict, has demonstrated that harsh, negative words can lead to permanent relational harm. Over a span of more than three decades, Gottman and his colleagues developed a method that can predict with over 90 percent accuracy whether a couple will eventually divorce. One of the indicators that Gottman and his colleagues observe is a few minutes of a videotaped argument.[4]

Gottman pays close attention when an argument escalates. Although virtually all couples—even happy ones—fight, Gottman's research shows that excessively sharp and negative responses usually foreshadow trouble. Disproportionate and searing verbal attacks, he has concluded, bode poorly for long-term relational sustainability.

The Neanderthal instinct urges us to overrespond when something upsets us. In addition to the personal and relational stress associated with harsh responses, there are five other negative consequences to responding with excessive force:[5]

1. **Excessive force alerts all Neanderthals in the vicinity.** When you send an overly strong message that you intend to stand your ground or when you push back too hard against an issue, you goad a similarly excessive—and almost certainly damaging—response from your conversational partner.

2. **Excessive force often produces the opposite of your goal.** People fight hard to maintain their autonomy and freedom from imposition, which is why many vigorous demands—*quit showing up late; stop yelling at me; don't date him*—often trigger the opposite reaction.

3. **Excessive force quickly loses effectiveness.** When you are identified as someone who overreacts, people will insulate themselves from the danger of your extreme reactions and will frequently isolate you.

4. **Excessive force prevents self-correction.** People will often self-correct when given the space to do so, but excessive force makes it harder for someone to walk back from or disclaim her words.

5. **Excessive force wastes your interpersonal capital.** Overreactions siphon away some of your goodwill account balance with others. As we've seen, you can't afford to have insufficient funds when a big mistake, major problem, or other traumatic event comes along and demands a significant expenditure of your accumulated goodwill.

The consequences of overreacting funnel us toward a single communication principle: *apply the least amount of interpersonal force and intensity necessary to accomplish your objectives.*

How do you know when you are in danger of overreacting or using more interpersonal force than necessary? Three warning signs can alert you. First, if your Neanderthal instinct overwhelms your communication conscience, you're more likely to overreact. Second, if you are talking so fast that your mind can't keep up or you're literally getting breathless, you are in a danger zone. And third, if you stop caring about what you are saying and start focusing only on proving your point or winning the argument, you are likely to apply too much interpersonal force.

Neutralizing Someone Else's Excessive Force

Conversational Matching

Of course, you aren't the only one who can sharply escalate a conversation. Hearing harsh and unexpected negative words is discombobulating and painful, but retaliation will only make the situation worse. The ability to neutralize verbal attacks is a challenging but essential tool for your communication toolkit. And the easiest way to neutralize someone else's excessive response is with *conversational matching*.

In a conversation, there's a natural momentum that moves people toward a similar tone, pace, and flow that broadly shapes overall communication.[6] This conversational matching exerts pressure throughout an interaction, moving intensity levels up or down as a conversation progresses.

If someone interjects harsh, accusatory words, she exerts pressure on the other party to match the conversation's elevated intensity level. Those retaliatory words further escalate the situation, and since the instigator was primed to fight in the first place, the interaction can quickly spiral out of control. This is how conversational matching usually works against us.

But it doesn't have to be this way. We could just as easily moderate our response when someone sharply escalates a situation, allowing the power of matching to exert downward pressure on the conversation's intensity level. As we've discussed, people often correct errors when given the opportunity to do so, and a neutralizing response provides the space for self-correction and uses conversational matching to remove some intensity from the interaction.

Picture an intensity dial that goes from 1 to 10. On the dial, 1 is the lowest and 10 is the highest. If you're in an interaction that's reading at 8 or above, you're in a relational danger zone; 3

and below are relatively safe. Resist your initial urge to respond to a level-8 verbal attack ("You blew the Gatorville contract! I can't believe it!") with retaliatory words that would match the danger zone intensity level. Instead, pull your punches by responding with something closer to a level-2 intensity ("I'm crushed that we lost Gatorville. I want to do whatever I can to make sure that something like this never happens again"). Often, your conversational partner will take your cue and respond with a lower-intensity response.

You shouldn't passively accept a negative conversation that starts on or escalates to a high-intensity level, and, as we'll discuss, you shouldn't accept harsh conversations too frequently either. Use the force of conversational matching when appropriate to intentionally lower the intensity level instead.

Four actions can help you use conversational matching to stabilize a conversation:

1. **Be serious.** Match your conversational partner's seriousness, but don't match the intensity. Although verbal attacks may take you by surprise, don't suggest that the attack was wrong, illogical, or stupid—no matter how strongly you may feel that way. Don't be glib or sarcastic. And don't laugh, no matter how ludicrous you think the accusation is, or raise your voice, no matter how upset you are. Show your conversational partner that you take her concerns seriously, even if you plan to reject the claims. Your first goal is to reduce the intensity level of the conversation. Demonstrate through your composure during your conversational turns that the root issue (if there is one) can be discussed at a lower, less divisive intensity level.

2. **Be focused.** Focus on what's happening (a verbal attack that you need to neutralize), not on what's being said. High-intensity attacks are usually inaccurate, emotional, and destructive. They may even be nonsensical. Instead of

trying to refute or address anything specific at this level, focus on lowering the whole conversation's intensity by using some of the neutralizing statements in the next section.

3. **Be boring.** Your words should be calm, controlled, and stabilizing. Don't add any new emotional material. Every time you speak, lower your volume and moderate your tone to reduce the conversation's intensity level. Refrain from any retaliatory responses, ignore the logic holes that you're dying to point out, and disregard any hypocrisy or foolishness you hear. In other words, be boring, and then . . .

4. **Be gone.** Once you reduce a conversation's intensity level, look for an exit. Safety is fleeting after a verbal attack—danger still lurks. So as soon as you realize that there's no substantive issue requiring a solution, extract yourself from the conversation as quickly as possible, perhaps after an apology, but definitely before additional damage is done. Even in cases where you still need to discuss a root issue, take a break in the conversation to support your intensity-reduction efforts. When you return, keep the focus on the issue and, as always, remember to contain.

The Neutralizing Two-Step:
Apology + Acknowledgment

Another highly effective way to neutralize harsh words is to respond with two things: an immediate apology and a statement acknowledging the other person's feelings.

"I'm sorry you're upset" (apology). "I didn't mean to make you feel that way" (acknowledgment of feelings).

Both parts are required. The immediate apology "gives" the other person something that isn't escalatory—that is, you give him an apology instead of the fight that he was probably expecting. And the acknowledgment of his feelings signals that you have received his message and that you are taking his feelings seriously.

Here are some other examples of the apology-acknowledgment neutralization tactic:

Intense statement. "This is the worst report I've ever read!"

Neutralizing response. "I'm sorry you don't like it. I didn't mean to upset you."

Intense statement. "I can't believe you did that! That's stupid!"

Neutralizing response. "I'm sorry you're upset. I didn't mean to make you feel that way."

Intense statement. "You contradict everything I say! It's driving me crazy!"

Neutralizing response. "I apologize. I didn't mean to make you feel that way."

This neutralizing tactic works because it is the fastest way to take the Neanderthal out of the room. It takes two to tangle; *there's no escalated interaction without your participation.* This approach forces a trade: your continued participation for a safer, more restrained interaction. If your conversational partner doesn't agree, then you withhold your participation and there's no interaction. All that's left to the Neanderthal is a lecture, and that's unappetizing to someone who came itching for a fight.

Besides, you won't let anyone lecture you very often anyway. Use the neutralizing tactic whenever you need to return a caustic conversation to civility, but don't accept repeated verbal attacks from anyone. If you find yourself neutralizing someone's harsh words frequently, you've got a relationship problem to address. Here's how.

Blast Me Twice, Shame on Me

Returning a conversation to civility by neutralizing provocative words is an important strategy to protect the underlying relationship when someone has a bad day and uncharacteristically lashes out at us. Sometimes a boss, under enormous pressure, snaps. Or a colleague misinterprets our words and reels off a zinger. Even the most disciplined among us has moments when the Neanderthal's voice slips through and we say something harsh and aggressive (even though we usually regret it).[7] But repeated incidences of harsh words directed at us are probable signs of a larger problem: someone who routinely uses words as weapons to exert relational control. The technical term for the behavior is *verbal aggression*; the common name is *bullying*.

There isn't a bully behind all sharp and insensitive words. But when one person repeatedly uses harsh words against another person, it's not the situation that's the problem; it's the verbally aggressive person. And it's a problem you must address if you are on the receiving end.

How will you know when you should treat harsh words as a serious relationship problem or when you should neutralize harsh words and then let them go? Paulo Coelho provides the best advice: "Everything that happens once can never happen again. But everything that happens twice will surely happen a third time."[8] Don't assume that you're dealing with problematic verbal aggression until you see it twice, but at that point it's safe to infer that you'll see it again and again unless you address it.

When one person speaks negatively and without restraint, the other person will have a difficult time believing there's safe ground for dialogue. This greatly reduces the opportunity for civilized communication and, if left unaddressed, will come to perpetuate a lopsided power-control dynamic in the relationship.

Verbal aggression will deteriorate your relationship if it gains a foothold. Relationships characterized by repeated verbal aggression are injured and may become impossible to repair. This is the first reason you need to *do something* if someone is consistently using harsh words against you.

The second reason to act on repeated verbal aggression is that bullying can sometimes be stopped with a single conversation. Treat this conversation like any other important one and develop a strategy using the preparation techniques outlined in Chapter 8 (the example there portrays an apartment manager who is confronting a verbally aggressive resident).

In addition, follow this advice when addressing repeated verbal aggression:

➤ **Pursue only one goal.** *Your only goal in confronting verbal aggression is to ensure that it never happens again.* Don't allow tangents to divert focus away from the single behavior—verbal aggression—that you are trying to extinguish.

➤ **Be timely.** Have the conversation as soon as you can after the incident, and use the harsh words as your example of the behavior that needs to stop. Wait for a private moment (it's best to have this conversation without an audience) and for your emotions to cool down a little bit, but try to have the conversation the same day as the incident. Waiting increases the likelihood that you might avoid the conversation indefinitely or that the other person will treat what you are saying as old news.

➤ **Be firm.** Tell the other person that the harsh words upset you (repeat the offending words verbatim), and ask him not to do this in the future. "Jim, it upset me when you said that I was an idiot for losing the Gatorville contract. I feel terrible about what happened, but I'd appreciate it if you'd not call me names or raise your voice at me in the future." Resist the urge to delve into the psychology of what happened. You want the behavior to stop, so stick to a simple restatement of the offending words and a request for the harsh comments to cease in the future. Give him an opportunity to reverse course, recant, or offer anything that resembles an apology. The conversation may be awkward, so don't look for a smooth apology. Any hint of remorse will work—take it and exit.

➤ **Contain, but don't exit early.** If the other person doesn't apologize and the conversation escalates, contain it, *but don't immediately look for an exit.* You need to stick around in this conversation to demonstrate that the verbally aggressive behavior isn't going to intimidate you. Besides, the reason we exit escalated conversations is to protect the underlying relationship, and here you are addressing a behavior that, if left unchecked, is likely to seriously injure or possibly dismantle the relationship. You need to stay in this conversation. Repeat the offending words again and ask the other person politely, but firmly, to communicate with you differently in the future. If you don't get some kind of apology or feel a hint of remorse after two or three attempts, exit the interaction. It's possible that you've made your point, but you aren't going to see any contrition (which is okay, because your sole goal is to prevent harsh words in the future).

If multiple attempts to stop verbally aggressive behavior are ineffective, you are on the short end of a lopsided relationship. Depending on your circumstances, dramatically reducing, or even eliminating, your exposure to the other person might be appropriate.

If the verbal aggressor is your boss, you might choose to delay the conversation until you can line up other work options, but you should eventually do something to address the behavior. If you truly can't talk to your boss about the behavior or if she blows you off when you raise the conversation, consider talking to your boss's supervisor about the problem, requesting a transfer, or accelerating your search for another job.[9]

With the exception of repeated verbal aggression, respond gently to excessive interpersonal force. Your most important relationships deserve restraint to prevent a destructive cycle of retaliatory attacks from knocking them to the ground. Smart communicators exercise restraint by applying the least amount of force necessary to resolve interpersonal conflict.

In the next chapter, we'll use our restraint skill again when we learn to change the way we think about change.

13

CHANGE YOUR CHANGE PLAN

DO LAST WHAT YOU WANT TO DO FIRST

When one of my clients initiated a corporate restructuring, the company offered Mary a major promotion into executive management. There was only one catch: her promotion was conditional on her ability to iron out differences with her colleague Jill. The two women had a long and antagonistic history, but would now have to work closely together.

I met with Mary to discuss the potential promotion. As soon as I mentioned Jill's name, Mary jumped right in. "Jill doesn't respect me and my opinions; that's why we don't get along. She doesn't listen to me, and she tries to embarrass me all the time. Let me tell you what she did last week . . ."

Mary continued talking for several minutes. When she stopped, I didn't say anything. "Well? What do you think?" she asked.

I told Mary that I couldn't help her until she quit blaming Jill and started looking for other ways to improve the relationship and get more of the productive communication she wanted. I didn't say anything else and there was a period of silence while Mary—known for her fiery personality—probably thought about giving me an earful.

But when she spoke again, she only said, "I'm not thrilled about having to work more closely with Jill, but I have to figure something out because I want this promotion."

Mary did what most of us do when we aren't getting the communication (or anything else) that we want; we blame the other person and try to force them to change. But blaming others and demanding that they change doesn't usually lead to more of the interactions we want. It leads to reciprocal finger-pointing, counterpressure, and usually a damaging escalation. Fortunately, there are three better ways to get the communication we want.

Stop Looking for the Click-to-Change Button

There's no button to get people to do what we want them to, especially if they're not ready. Research by James Prochaska, Carlo DiClemente, and John Norcross suggests that people typically progress through behavioral change at their own pace, moving through a series of steps over time and often repeating steps before they make significant change.[1] Prochaska, DiClemente, and Norcross's Stages of Change model (modified for our use) describes this progression, with insights about what you can expect from people and how you can best support them at each stage.

Stages of Change

> **Precontemplation stage.** People in the precontemplation stage are not thinking about change in the immediate future, which researchers usually define as within the next

six months. Advocating or agitating for change in this precontemplation stage is almost certain to be counterproductive. Just wait. They aren't even ready to *think* about change.

- **Contemplation stage.** Here people begin to think about changing within the next six months. It's appropriate for you to serve as a sounding board and to provide encouragement and support in this stage ("I think that might be a good idea" or "That sounds like a sensible plan"), but don't push for them to act until they're ready. This is where Mary, from the earlier example, was when I first met with her. She was out of the precontemplation stage and had been thinking about her conflict with Jill for months. Additionally, Mary's conditional promotion provided the spark she needed to move to the preparation stage.
- **Preparation stage.** In this stage, people commit to initiate change in the next month or earlier. Your encouragement here can be especially valuable. Give them positive feedback every time they talk to you about the impending change, and reiterate your support occasionally. At the end of our first meeting, I asked Mary to put a plan together for improving her working relationship with Jill and bring it to our next meeting. This assignment fit where Mary was mentally—almost, but not quite ready to act—and gave her an opportunity to develop her own change plan.
- **Action stage.** In the action stage, people implement their change and set new behavioral patterns for the next three to six months. Provide continual support and encouragement here to help them cement the new path. Give positive feedback when you see manifestations of the new behavior and when milestones are reached, and prop them up when they stumble. It took Mary a week to

come up with her plan. Her first action was to convene a meeting with Jill about reshaping their working relationship. I helped facilitate the first two meetings until they were comfortable with the process. Progress was uneven for over a month, as Mary worked to be less reactive in her relationship with Jill.

➤ **Maintenance stage.** In this stage, a new behavior has been established for at least six months. Periodically highlight and celebrate the positive aspects of the change, and provide support to help people recover from any setbacks. Backsliding is a possibility, but the change effort has been initially successful because they have maintained the change for six or more months. Mary called me a few times after the new relationship was established when she had concerns about reverting to old, unproductive behaviors, but she never needed much more than reassurance to stay the course. Mary and Jill never became best friends, but they did find a way to get more of the productive communication they needed. With their relationship sufficiently improved, Mary got her promotion.

Our efforts to force communication change (or any other type of change) on someone else often fail because when we demand that someone act right away, we ignore a person's need to work through the first three change steps. No matter how carefully we communicate what we want, the other person often resists.

Instead of asking for change on our schedule, look for and encourage signs of progress when someone is moving through the Stages of Change. Although personal change is difficult, people are often aware of and are actively trying to address their communication (and other) failings. Jim knows that his sarcastic tongue gets him in trouble, Betty is aware that she's sometimes too quick to dismiss your ideas, and Sam realizes that he's prone to overreaction.

When you catch a behavior that's in the direction you want, positive feedback can encourage the other person to continue through the Stages of Change. Thank Jim when he stops a criticism in midsentence, express your appreciation to Betty for hearing out your thoughts, and tell Sam after a productive collaboration that you enjoyed working with him.

People seldom change on demand, and by ignoring this reality we set ourselves up for likely failure.

But I don't try to change people on my schedule, you might be protesting. Think again. You probably ask people to stop or start doing something—to change—more often than you realize. And even if you're not *intentionally* pushing change, expedient communication can make your messages sound like a demand to change something, do something, or stop something immediately.

Hasty e-mails and curt text messages can't carry your tone of voice or easily convey your positive intentions, and so it's easier for others to misread your messages as demands (which people love to reject) instead of requests (which they are more likely to consider). Expediency also makes us jump into conversations faster, contradict people more often, and push harder for our terms without laying interpersonal groundwork first. We skip small things like openings (*Dear Sarah*) and closings (*Sincerely yours*) and rush into our message, thereby subtly reinforcing the idea that we are really making demands instead of requests.

Sending a text to Scott about a new deadline ("Can I get your report by 4 p.m.?") is more likely to trigger Scott's resistance than a phone call, where you would have the space to tell him why the deadline moved up, to acknowledge the disruption to his schedule, and to express your appreciation for his help.

Without those interpersonal details, your expedient text could trigger multiple issues. Scott might get upset because this is the second time in as many weeks you've inserted yourself into his schedule. He might feel like you're ordering him around, even though the two of you are peers. He might be stressed out about another deadline that he can't ignore. He might be worried about something at home. He might think that you're overreacting by moving the deadline up. He might not be inclined to help you because of something you did or didn't do in the past, because of the way he feels about you in general, or just because he doesn't want to. Without a higher-order interpersonal channel, it's hard to gauge, and possibly address, what's bothering him.

Asking people to stop, start, or change anything is almost always better communicated by synchronous, higher-order communication channels that allow you to monitor verbal and nonverbal cues, decrease reflexive resistance, and, if needed, adapt on the fly based on the feedback you receive.

Asynchronous communication channels, like text messages and e-mail, don't have the capacity to easily handle the interpersonal factors that come with many situations. The real issue is not how much digital bandwidth our devices can process; it's how little interpersonal capacity they can readily manage.

We know this intuitively, because when a text message gets misconstrued or an e-mail gets mangled in transmission, most of us reach for a synchronous channel like the phone or a face-to-face conversation to straighten things out. But we usually don't switch to a more time- and energy-intensive synchronous channel until there's a problem.

People don't like it when we pressure them to change their communication or any other behavior, and many of our expedient communication practices make sensible requests seem like imposing demands.

Change the Situation

In 1971, Philip Zimbardo conducted an experiment that would become famous. Using some vacant office space in Stanford University's psychology department, he simulated a prison and recruited untrained undergraduates from the area as guards and prisoners. Shortly after the experiment started, Zimbardo noticed that many of the guards were verbally harassing the prisoners. The harassment quickly escalated into more direct hazing. The prisoners' sleep was disrupted, they were made to do exercises to the point of exhaustion and clean toilets with their bare hands, and solitary confinement was doled out to unruly prisoners. The simulation became so "real" that Zimbardo ended the two-week experiment after only six days.[2]

The study, called the Stanford Prison Experiment, demonstrated that putting "normal" people in unfavorable circumstances (in the case of the prison, the existence of asymmetrically powerful roles, with little oversight of and no formal training for the guards) can lead to undesirable outcomes. Zimbardo's experiment was a vivid contradiction to the human inclination to assign blame for bad behavior to only "a few bad apples." If the barrel itself is rotten, even good apples have a tendency to sour.[3]

In another research study, when seminary students were told that they were running late to deliver a brief speech, their inclination to stop and help a person in distress was dramatically reduced. This was true even when they were on the way to deliver remarks *about the Good Samaritan parable.*[4]

Situational changes—even relatively small ones—can significantly alter human behavior. In communication situations, people readily change their speech patterns to converge with or diverge from various people and groups.[5] Someone born in Brooklyn but living in Los Angeles may talk like a West Coast beach boy 99 percent of the time, but when he returns home or when he talks with old New York friends, the original accent returns (convergence). Or he might slip back into the East Coast accent if he wanted to highlight his New York roots in a group of California natives (divergence). I act one way with my boss, another way with my friends, and another way with my mom. I talk one way at a restaurant, another way in a company meeting, and yet another way on a sales call. In organizations, situations shape behaviors and can encourage or discourage positive behaviors like mentoring, volunteering, and assuming extra-role behaviors.[6]

So what does all this mean for us and our quest for better communication? The examples help us to remember that situations—people, places, and events—exert a great influence on our behavior. Likewise, structural changes in how we communicate— quick, cheap, and easy or thoughtful and deliberate—change our behavior.

Just as it is possible to construct a prison that brings out the worst in guards or squash helping behaviors in would-be preachers by changing a deadline, we can change how people interact with us by changing the underlying conditions of the situation and by changing our communication with them.

Change the Underlying Conditions

Let's say your colleague Sarah never lets you finish a sentence without jumping in with questions, criticisms, or ideas of her own. Naturally, this upsets you and makes you feel like she doesn't listen. Instead of thinking about all that's wrong with Sarah and how she needs to change, ask yourself a different question: *How can I change the underlying conditions of the interactions I have with Sarah so she's more likely to listen?*

You want Sarah to listen to you—that's the specific communication behavior you want more of—and there's plenty you can do to affect that.

To get good at changing underlying conditions, you'll need to think more like an experimenter (*I wonder what happens if I try this?*) and less like a drill sergeant (*Change now, private!*). Think about the conditions that surround you and Sarah. What were your best interactions with her? How do other people who interact favorably with her behave?

Then try different things to find out what works best. For example, what happens if you send an e-mail first (so she can't interrupt) and then follow up with a face-to-face conversation? Are there certain times of the day when Sarah is more likely to listen? Does she interrupt you more frequently when other people are around? Is she more relaxed (and more likely to listen) away from the office? What happens when you talk to her over lunch? Is she a more focused and better listener when she's away from her computer or when her phone is quiet?

Test different situational variables and see if the result is better communication. If you find one or two things that work fairly consistently—perhaps Sarah's more relaxed and willing to listen first thing in the morning or when she's away from her computer—plan your interactions around these favorable conditions whenever possible.

Change Your Communication

In addition to changing underlying conditions, how you choose to communicate with Sarah also exerts a significant force on how the two of you interact. People are keenly impacted by social cues, which is a major reason why conversations often converge in pace, tone, and intensity.[7] My conversational actions influence you, and vice versa, which makes our communication behaviors powerful factors in shaping our interactions.

To encourage Sarah to listen more, for instance, you might try to repeat your key points during the conversation. Or you could talk softly so she has to listen harder just to understand what you're saying. Speaking softly might also cue Sarah that what you are saying is important. You could strip everything but the essential points from your dialogue or ask her for one minute of uninterrupted time to talk at the beginning of the conversation. And so on. Again, experiment with the variables to see what works. Each situation offers different ways you can change your communication to get more of the communication you want in return.

Let's take another example. I once helped a new manager, Sally, to communicate more effectively with a manager named Rick. Rick was an emotional person, and Sally was having a hard time troubleshooting work issues with him. As soon as the conversation touched on something he was responsible for, Rick would react forcefully and shut down the conversation. Everyone else steered clear of Rick, but Sally had to collaborate with him on multiple issues. And neither Sally nor Rick would ever be fired: Sally had been with the company from its humble beginnings, and Rick was related to one of the owners. They were stuck with each other.

Sally and I knew that Rick wouldn't change, so we looked instead for steps Sally could take to improve their interactions. We quickly determined that the only way to have a nontrivial conversation with Rick was one-on-one (he was hyperdefensive in groups) and either face-to-face or over the phone (Sally needed a synchronous channel to be able to hear his voice to pick up on cues that Rick was getting uncomfortable).

Rick's day-to-day moods were also heavily impacted by what was going on at home. He spoke freely about the challenges and the joys of being a single parent, which made it feasible for Sally to determine, without asking, more optimal times to talk to him.

Through trial and error, we discovered that Rick was particularly sensitive to questions. Sally's questions couldn't contain a trace of accusation, or Rick would shut the conversation down. Sally learned to ask her questions in less threatening ways ("Could you help me think through why our Wichita Falls store is calling about its supply order?" versus "Why is Wichita Falls complaining again about its supply order?"), and this led to the observation that if Sally let Rick say whatever he wanted to early in the conversation, she could usually contribute her thoughts later. Finally, Sally determined that once Rick got defensive and started shutting down the dialogue, there was no saving the conversation. She needed to abandon the discussion for another day.

These experiments and observations led Sally to find the underlying conditions that were most likely to facilitate the kinds of results-oriented conversations she needed with Rick: one-on-one, synchronous conversations, preferably when things weren't tumultuous in Rick's home life. And Sally changed her communication to encourage better dialogue in return by letting Rick talk first, by asking nonthreatening questions, and by not continuing conversations when Rick became defensive.

Sally's techniques don't work every time; she still calls me occasionally for ideas after failed conversations. And Rick's personality didn't change in the slightest. But by finding and using favorable underlying conditions and by altering her communication, Sally found ways to get more of the communication she needed from Rick.

Climb Aboard the Straight-Talk Express Last

If you don't get more of the communication you want by encouraging someone through the Stages of Change, by changing the underlying conditions of the interaction, or by changing your own communication, you'll need to have a direct conversation with the other person.

As someone who makes his living helping people and organizations improve their communication, I'm a big supporter of having direct, meaningful conversations when necessary. But there's a mountain of caution in those last two words.

Multiple forces encourage us to think we need more direct conversations—like interventions or confrontations—than we really do. As we've already seen, the hypercommunicating digital environment propels us into more marginally important conversations, and we often erroneously inflate the seriousness of those discussions. Our Neanderthal instincts see threats to overreact to everywhere. Our human flaws cause us to exaggerate how much someone else is to blame and minimize our own culpability. Our emotions cause our words to trump our goals.

And let's not forget the three fundamental properties of communication: powerful, imperfect, and asymmetrical. Our words matter (power). Errors happen when people interact (imperfect). We can destroy in seconds what it took years to build (asymmetrical).

Add to all this the fact that our attempts to change someone else usually fail, and it's easy to see why we should try everything else in our communication toolkit before directly confronting another person with a negative issue.

But sometimes we do have to directly address problematic behaviors that aren't improving through other strategies. At the root of a conversation like this is negative feedback. Something isn't right, and you're going to point that out in an attempt to alter the behavior.

Negative feedback is hard to deliver effectively, because people don't want to hear it. Even the most well-intentioned feedback is often reflexively perceived as personal criticism. You say to Jim, "I think we'd be more productive if I could tell you what I'm thinking about our key clients more often," but what Jim hears is "You're the reason the Gatorville project failed" or "You're a bad listener." When people perceive feedback as criticism, conversations can escalate quickly as the receiver pushes back against the unwanted and threatening advice.

Delivering negative feedback is a tough, but essential, higher-order communication skill that usually comes with a relational cost. Because it's easier not to say anything, a great deal of potentially helpful feedback is not delivered.[8]

But feedback is too important to abandon, and some issues need to be faced with a direct conversation in order to avoid a major problem or to provide crucial missing information. Our feedback might even, in exceptional cases, save a job or a marriage.

Starting a negative conversation is often the hardest part, since you need to overcome the other person's tendencies to reflexively treat negative feedback as personal criticism and immediately tune out your message. If you want to give negative feedback to a peer (or someone you have no formal authority over), the most effective way to disarm this reflexive resistance is to ask for permission to deliver the feedback: "I've noticed something that I think is causing you trouble. Would you like my observations about it?" If you don't get permission, let the feedback go. If you get permission, proceed directly to the issue: "I'm noticing that you are inadvertently cutting off your boss during staff meetings," or "I don't think Janet understands what you're saying during staff meetings. You seem to be talking faster than she can process your words."

If you have formal authority over the other person, don't ask for permission to deliver negative feedback—it's your job, and the other person really doesn't have a choice to decline (which makes asking for permission a faulty question). Move right into the conversation: "Mary, I need to talk with you about something that I'm observing when we meet with clients," or "Mary, we need to talk for a few minutes about something that I'm seeing during our client meetings." You can also use this procedure when you aren't the boss but when the behavior in question is directly impacting you.

Whether you have formal authority over someone or not, you can reduce some of the resistance people feel toward negative feedback with the following five guidelines:

1. **Have a simple message and provide examples.** Decide precisely what you're going to say and make that message the conversation's focal point. Your conversational goal when delivering negative feedback is to get your message across with the least amount of collateral damage (damage to the underlying relationship or to the person's internal motivation) as possible.

   Keep your feedback specific to the situation, avoiding pervasive (broad and expansive) statements. Effective feedback always points to a solution or a way to succeed. Bill doesn't get much that's useful from a blanket criticism that he's a bad presenter, but knowing that he had way too many slides at today's client meeting may help. Most people can work with specific, incident-related negative feedback, but pervasive feedback is demoralizing and can throttle a person's internal motivation. After all, Bill can look for ways to be more organized and concise in his next client pitch, but if he's just a bad presenter, how does he fix that? Similarly, Jane can't do anything with the criticism that she's bad with people, but concrete examples of her constant interruptions of me, Sarah, and Steve during our meeting yesterday may point the way toward better interactions between her and the staff.

   If you don't have a specific instance of the behavior you want to address, you aren't ready to have the conversation. Without an example, your interaction can quickly devolve into unhelpful generalities and allow the other person to easily (and possibly correctly) dismiss your feedback as groundless. A simple, specific message with an example or two to illustrate the problematic behavior will help you achieve your conversational goal—getting your message across with the least amount of collateral damage—more than any other approach.

2. **Discuss the incident or behavior, not the person.**[9] Don't talk about what the person *is* (a terrible presenter or bad with people); instead, talk about what he *did* (showed too many slides on Thursday or interrupted too frequently yesterday). To reduce resistance to your message, have the conversation one-on-one and in private, which will help the other person feel safer in the conversation. And as always, contain throughout the discussion should escalation occur.

3. **Separate intentions from perceptions.** If you want to preempt some reflexive resistance, or if you're finding a lot of opposition to your message, you can give your feedback in the following way: *I know you probably didn't intend for X, but that's how I perceived it (or that's how it felt to me).* For example, "Jim, I know you probably didn't intend to cut me off in the meeting, but that's what I perceived today," "Bill, I know you don't intend to ignore my ideas, but that's how I feel when you don't let me finish my sentences," and "Sarah, I know that you don't mean to confuse our clients, but that's what I perceived today."

4. **Don't dilute your message with a pile of positive statements.** Have you ever heard that when you give feedback you should offer two positive statements for every negative one? Disregard that advice, because an avalanche of positivity will dilute your message and may confuse the other person *(Am I in trouble? What's with all the compliments? What's this conversation really about?).* As long as you're talking about an incident and not about the person (see the

earlier point about discussing the behavior, not the person), you are already doing more to protect the underlying relationship and the internal motivation of the recipient than a dozen positive comments will do.

5. **Don't worry if the initial conversation is short.** After you have crafted a worthwhile message and delivered it clearly, don't allow yourself to fall into hours of meandering conversation. Don't let your message—the reason for the conversation in the first place—get suffocated as extraneous topics are heaped on top of it. Sometimes people need two conversations: one just to get the information and another to respond, discuss, and potentially move toward a resolution of some kind. Listen to what the other person has to say, and if the initial discussion doesn't resolve the underlying issue, schedule time for another discussion.

To get more of the productive and meaningful communication we want, we should first pull on the levers that work best.

For better communication, we also need to ignore the pervasive digital age notion that all topics are fair game. That's the subject of our next chapter.

14

TAKE THINGS OFF THE TABLE

JUST BECAUSE YOU CAN TALK ABOUT SOMETHING DOESN'T MEAN THAT YOU SHOULD

stopped talking about politics 15 years ago, on the day I read my first research study about identity.

Identity is how people answer the question *Who am I?*, and their answers reveal their cherished, core beliefs. *I'm an American. I'm a feminist. I'm a Cherokee. I'm a teacher. I'm a veteran. I'm a writer. I'm a hard worker. I'm a Democrat. I'm a Republican. I'm a family man. I'm a company man. I'm a lawyer. I'm a mother.* The way we define ourselves—capturing our core and most cherished beliefs—is vitally important. It's part of how we establish our sense of self, and it shapes the way that we communicate about the topics that matter most to us.

That identity study helped me understand that politics, a topic I didn't get too excited about and wasn't defined by, was enormously important to many people in my life. I'd been breezing through conversations about the elections that year, making jokes and lighthearted observations about something that I suddenly realized was extremely meaningful to others. I was just talking. They were talking about who they were. The mismatch was treacherous.

From a communication perspective, understanding identity matters because it's how we come to know a person deeply and meaningfully. Some of our most important conversations, with some of the most important people in our lives, will be identity-related discussions. That's the good news. The bad news is that the most damaging conversations of our lives are also usually about identity topics. Just because we can talk about something doesn't mean that we always should.

If I speak negatively about something that another person holds dear, escalation happens faster and with more intensity because the stakes are higher. The damage will be more severe and more difficult to repair, if it can be repaired.

We've heard for decades that it's bad form to talk about sex, religion, and politics—the classic identity triad. The passage of time hasn't altered this advice. Some topics, with some people, should be approached with caution.

Over a hundred years ago, Mark Twain noted that "it is by the goodness of God that in our country we have those three unspeakably precious things: freedom of speech, freedom of conscience, and the prudence never to practice either of them."[1]

Unfortunately, the anything-goes ethos of the digital age prevents this elementary communication lesson from sticking. Our gadgets and a proliferation of instant communication opportunities didn't erase our identity beliefs, but they did encourage a more relaxed approach to the topics we discuss. Unless we start exercising greater caution and restraint around identity-related topics, our relationships may suffer explosive consequences.

There's TNT in Identity

Identity is, in some ways, like a deck of cards representing an assortment of formative experiences and deeply held feelings. *I'm a hard worker* (queen of diamonds), *I'm a great salesperson* (ace of clubs), *I'm a mom* (and so on), *I'm a pilot, I'm a triathlete, I'm a cancer survivor*. We make our identity "hand" from the cards we hold.

Our identities are shaped by many factors, including family, upbringing, life experience, religion, worldview, and work. A person's identity reflects her core beliefs and how she sees herself in the world.

Common identities include:

- ➤ **Where you are from.** American, Polish, Chinese, Texan, Hawaiian

- ➤ **Core beliefs.** Republican/Democrat; conservative liberal/libertarian; pro-life/pro-choice; Christian/Jewish/Muslim/Hindu/Buddhist/atheist; environmentalist; vegetarian/vegan; peace/human rights/community activist

- ➤ **What you believe about yourself.** Hard worker; honest; good at my job; caring; a good listener; dependable; animal lover

Identity-related topics are combustible because they touch on our self-image and self-esteem.[2] Identity violations are not just conversational gaffes; they are often seen as rejections of the other person's core beliefs. Discussions about identity issues can be very personal.

This doesn't mean that identity-related conversations are always forbidden. When your identity beliefs are in general alignment with another person's, you can talk about them all day long without special precautions (although you'll still want to contain conversational escalations, as always). And if neither conversational partner's identity beliefs are wrapped up in a particular topic, discussing it is probably safe. That's why two people who aren't that interested in politics can usually discuss different political viewpoints without incident.

But there are three cases where you need to be very careful around identity-related topics: when you hold divergent or opposing identity views to those of your conversational partner; when one person's identity is wrapped up in the topic but the other person's isn't; and when you discuss identity-related topics through mass communication channels, because reaching more people means there are more identity beliefs to consider.

Don't assume that you know what your conversational partner's identity views are, and don't assume that she knows all of yours either. We expect that people we identify with in one way are like us in most other ways (for example, we expect people who share our religious beliefs to also share our political beliefs and our views on parenting), but the truth is more complicated.

Studies do show that your network will include more people who are like you across demographic variables and core beliefs when compared with the population at large.[3] African-American women have more African-American women in their network, Catholics have more Catholics, vegans have more vegans, etc. But it's also true that almost no one ever sees us across all the contexts of our identity. Most people only see a few of our identity cards. My relatives rarely, if ever, see my work identity. Most of my clients don't see my family identity. My mom knows things about me that my old platoon sergeant on Facebook doesn't and vice versa.

The more we like certain people and the more we interact with them, the more we come to believe they know us accurately.[4] This causes a gap between how well we *think* people know us and how well they actually do, which is exacerbated by the fact that humans are complicated, contradictory, and dynamic. We change our minds. We follow our hearts. We might not like something tomorrow that we like today. But we still expect that people we like will have a good understanding of who we are. You can see how this is a setup for problems.

My friend Sarah is a vegan, is pro-life, and is a lifelong yoga practitioner. Her husband, Bill, is a military officer from the Deep South. Politics is an identity belief for both of them, but if you had to guess their political affiliations, you'd probably go astray. Bill votes straight-ticket Democrat (reflecting his birth family's core beliefs), while Sarah tends to vote Republican (she's a libertarian). There are many cards in people's identity deck, but we usually only see a handful of them.

And people also add and remove cards in their hand over time. At this very moment, people throughout my network are reversing course on ideas that I didn't even know they had, accumulating experiences that are fundamentally changing their views of themselves and the world around them, and falling in and out of love with people, places, and beliefs. I still think that Matt from high school is the same scamp that he was back in the 1980s, even though he just became a grandfather. I assume that Jill in accounting is the same as the day I met her, even though she's changed churches, changed husbands, and seen her kids off to college in the last two years.

For many years, the fact that most people in our network only knew about a few of our identity cards wasn't a big deal. We saw co-workers in the office, immediate family at home, friends on weekends, and more distant family on vacation.

And then—along came the Internet.

Who Are These People?

Digital communication devices generally, and social media platforms in particular, have allowed us to see more of people's identity cards. This sounds like a good idea—we'll get to know people better—but more knowledge doesn't always bring people closer together.

Seeing more of a person's identity has disrupted, to varying degrees, our networks. Facebook reveals the fringe beliefs of a family member. A forwarded e-mail reveals way too much about a coworker's innermost thoughts. The Twitter feed of a client betrays a fondness for late nights in rowdy places.

Where identity is concerned, people are more attentive when your identity beliefs are incongruent with theirs. Mass disclosures often work against us, as every incongruent identity-related post gives people on the other side of an issue evidence that you are different from them, while congruent posts are just another piece of redundant information for the people in alignment with you. If you, too, like late nights in rowdy places, your client's midnight tweets probably don't make much of impact. But if his late-night tweets offend your sensibilities, they're more likely to garner your attention and make an impression.

Too much impulsive disclosure can upset the people who are most important to your work and personal life. The people closest to you want to believe that, in the big ways (meaning, in terms of their identity beliefs), they are similar to you. What you share with them isn't necessarily harmless self-expression; it may be disturbing evidence of your differences. They may even see it as a rejection of who they are.[5]

Does this mean that we should abandon the Internet, stop posting anything on social media, and never talk about identity issues? No, no, and no.

Go ahead and post about the great BBQ ribs you ate for lunch. Just don't write that eating the ribs made you realize how clueless vegetarians are. The first case is harmless self-expression and sharing something you enjoyed, but the second encroaches on the identity beliefs of others in your network. And this is true even if you don't think there are vegetarians in your network. Your high school chum who used to love hamburgers only eats tofu burgers now. Down the hall from your cubicle, Jim is weeping at this very moment while watching a YouTube video about factory farming, and Uncle Billy is about to get the word from his doctor that his heart's going to explode unless he locates the vegetable aisle.

All I'm recommending is some good, old-fashioned caution. Be thoughtful whenever you discuss identity issues because of the sensitive nature of core beliefs. And be especially careful on mass communication platforms because there are many more deeply held beliefs to consider. Failure to exercise caution around identity-related topics can lead to a relational explosion.

Boom Goes the Dynamite

As a graduate student, I once gave a lecture to over 500 undergraduates. After class, a female student handed me a note and hurried away before I could see who she was. I wondered if I had finally received one of the undergraduate love notes that are a staple of grad school folklore.

It turned out to be anything but. I had offended the student during part of my presentation when I poked fun at myself for a social error by saying that I was "socially retarded." The student's note explained that her younger sister was actually—not socially—retarded. I felt terrible that my use of the word *retarded* encroached on the student's core beliefs (about her family and about people with disabilities), hurt her feelings, and detracted from the lesson's message.

I was lucky because I received *discreet* and *immediate* negative feedback about my identity violation. The student's response was face-saving (imagine the student confronting me during the question and answer session instead) and self-containing (the incident ended automatically when the student handed me the note and walked away). It was also very effective. The timeliness of that feedback allowed me to make immediate changes to avoid future violations. I haven't used the word *retarded* since.

In spite of the seriousness of identity violations, people often don't report them because they are so sensitive. I conservatively assumed that at least 10 other students were offended by my words that day.

People may not confront you after an identity violation for a variety of reasons. Perhaps you are the boss and they don't think they can tell you. It could be that you have hurt them so deeply that they turn inward and dismiss you. Or maybe they are skilled at controlling their emotional reactions. When someone abruptly starts treating you differently or if a trusted third party tells you that you have offended someone, it's likely that you committed an identity violation.

If you commit an identity violation, regardless of how you learn about it, repair the damage by apologizing sincerely and immediately, because violations often get worse over time as the other person ruminates on the offense. After repairing the damage, be sure to avoid the core belief you violated in the future to prevent another detonation.

Let's say a conversation with Jim about a missed deadline explodes because he perceives it as an affront to his dependability, a core identity issue with him. Your job is to stop talking and start apologizing. Don't worry about your original conversational message (you probably made your point, albeit in a problematic way), and don't concern yourself with whether or not you are "right" (this is a tangential triviality when the underlying relationship is taking on damage). Repair the relational damage with an apology, and exit the conversation.

Obvious Cautionary Topics

The Triad: Sex, Religion, and Politics

As we discussed earlier, sex, religion, and politics are the perennial triad of conversational flashpoints; they are private, intimate subjects that can alienate people like few other topics can.

Even when you think you are on the same side of the discussion as your conversational partners, there is no guarantee of safety. Like-minded groups have a tendency to migrate toward more extreme opinions over time while punishing variance from group norms.[6] This means that the political discussion group (or environmental group, concerned taxpayers' group, or whatever) you joined is likely to move toward one end of the spectrum over time and that your more moderate views, if they manage to stay constant, will eventually be considered out of step with the group's beliefs.

A discussion about faith or sexuality might seem benign to you, like politics did for me, but for someone whose core identity is wrapped up in her beliefs, talking about these issues is usually intimate and personal. This mismatch can cause problems if your conversational partner believes you're trivializing a vital issue.

Of course, there are instances when these three topics are less volatile (but still sensitive)—talking about sex with your spouse or partner isn't something to avoid, even if the conversation might be tricky, and you might talk at length and without incident about your religious beliefs or your politics with a few close friends or colleagues. But the general rule holds: just because you can talk about a topic with someone doesn't mean that you always should.

Just ask former U.S. President Jimmy Carter, who agreed to a *Playboy* interview as he was entering the homestretch of the 1976 race for the White House. Carter was trying to allay concerns about his strict, straitlaced Southern Baptist image in order to bolster his appeal to young voters.

He must have known the interview was likely to raise a number of sensitive topics, and he managed to steer clear of controversy for most of the time. But the gulf between *most* and *all* almost torpedoed his chances for the White House.

The final question—when the reporters were literally on their way out the door—was a softball: did he think that he had been able to reassure voters through this interview that his religious beliefs would not make him a rigid president?[7]

Carter's response was long, detailed, and uncontroversial until he said this:

> *I try not to commit a deliberate sin. I recognize that I'm going to do it anyhow, because I'm human and I'm tempted. And Christ set almost impossible standards for us. Christ said, "I tell you that anyone who looks on a woman with lust has in his heart already committed adultery." I've looked on a lot of women with lust. I've committed adultery in my heart many times.[8]*

Unbelievably, Carter had pulled off a bad-topic trifecta: A *political* candidate answers a *religious* question by talking about *sex*.

It's easy to see that Carter was attempting to show that he was human and fallible like everyone else. But he bungled the execution. Writing about the incident years later, Carter said the *Playboy* interview almost cost him the election, and he was right.[9] In opinion polls conducted immediately following publication of the *Playboy* interview, Carter lost a staggering 15 percentage points, placing him in a statistical dead heat with the incumbent Gerald Ford, the man who had controversially pardoned Richard Nixon.[10] Suddenly, Carter didn't seem so presidential.

Family

The phrase *your momma* has triggered many a schoolyard scuffle, and for good reason—unwanted comments about someone's family from an "outsider" often create identity explosions.

Tread lightly when your conversational partner criticizes his family, even when he seems to be encouraging you to pile on the abuse. Don't add any substantive comments. As an outsider, you just don't have that prerogative.

This includes your in-laws. In a marriage or a romantic relationship, family discussions are very tricky. You aren't exactly an outsider to your spouse's family, but you didn't grow up in it, either. Caution is your safest course of action during cross-family discussions. Think twice before criticizing *anyone's* family.

It's usually safe to talk about positive events in someone's family life, like new babies, upcoming anniversaries, kids' soccer leagues, and birthdays. Similarly, sincere expressions of sympathy for the loss of a loved one or following an accident are usually appreciated.

Love and Money

No list of obviously sensitive conversational topics would be complete without a discussion of your heart and your wallet.

Let your exes live safely in your memory, not in your conversations. Talking about old flames with anyone, including your current romantic interest, is usually a terrible idea.

When people experience a trigger (learning about an old flame), they can't help but feel the emotion associated with it (usually jealousy and sadness). Your current partner might be sophisticated enough to exert self-control over an emotional response, but you are almost certainly making someone you love today feel sad when you talk about someone you loved yesterday.

Be discreet about how much money you have (or don't have) to anyone except your spouse or your financial advisor. People often have widely divergent views of money. It's all-important to some people, a necessary evil to others, and the root of all evil to others. And money talk triggers comparisons, creating an unnecessary distance and, worse, potentially triggering envy.

Hidden Minefields: Core Identities That Are Harder to Discern

Some identity-related topics are just as volatile as the topics discussed earlier, but they may be harder to detect and therefore harder to avoid.

A project manager might have a core belief that she should never miss a deadline because punctuality is part of her identity. A teacher may never give up on a student who is still trying to succeed because of her core belief that every student deserves help. An auto mechanic may never leave the shop until it's clean and ready for the next day because tidiness is a core belief that he learned from his family. These identity concerns may not be obvious until you try telling the teacher to stop bothering with the failing student or suggest to the project manager that missing a deadline is no big deal, at which time you may inadvertently stumble into an identity violation.

When you're getting to know someone, ask yourself five questions to help identify less obvious identity issues:

1. **What is his background?** Look to both personal and work history. Where was he born? What schools did he attend? What's his field of expertise? Draw reasonable inferences: veterans probably support the troops, graduates probably like their alma mater, and teachers probably think education is important. Not everything will be an identity clue, of course, but the more you know, the more likely you are to spot core beliefs.

2. **What is she displaying?** What's on the wall? What do her bumper stickers say? Who are in the pictures displayed on her desk or online?[11] Identity isn't only about family—some people are so connected to a job, a sports team, a university, a locale, or a company, that those things are a part of their identity.

3. **What is he wearing?** Clothes and jewelry sometimes contain words or symbols hinting at core issues. Someone wearing a pink breast cancer ribbon might be signaling a close encounter with the disease, people with POW/MIA car magnets may have a military connection, and phrases or logos on t-shirts can sometimes reveal identity. Tattoos may suggest identity beliefs (like *I love momma* or *Death before dishonor*), but don't overreach. A dragon leaping over a unicorn is probably not telling you much about the essence of a person.

4. **What groups does she affiliate with?** How and where does she spend her free time? What voluntary associations does she make (civic groups, places of worship, nonprofit programs, or political organizations)? Someone who volunteers with a particular group (political, environmental, community, women's issues, or children's issues) is probably offering a strong clue about her core beliefs.

5. **What issues elicit strong emotions?** What things make him express love, joy, or anger? What does he get upset about? Strong emotional expressions can sometimes be indicators of underlying identity issues, and forceful, passionate statements often represent core beliefs.

It's best to exercise caution in identity-related conversations when you and another person have opposing identity views or when you're communicating with a number of people (which increases the likelihood of divergent identity views). Let the other person talk freely (this will help prevent him from thinking that you are trivializing an important issue), and then choose your own words carefully. Whatever you do, don't challenge a core belief, and balance the need to let him express himself with the need to bring identity-related conversations to a close.

SLOW for Sensitive Conversations

Although exercising caution where core beliefs enter a conversation is a smart policy, there are times when we need to originate an identity-related conversation at work. For example, we might need to talk about a direct report's performance, which touches on competence (an identity-related issue for most people). Or we might have to talk to coworkers about missing deadlines, counsel subordinates about their poor client interactions, or let someone go for poor performance. At home, we may have to talk to our spouse about her wayward cousin who's living in our basement, talk to our siblings about an aging parent, or talk to a good friend who has started bad-mouthing our in-laws. When these and other sensitive situations come up, prepare for the conversation and use the acronym SLOW (slow down, lose the length, orient to the context, and welcome a response) to keep the discussion civilized and to minimize the likelihood that an identity explosion makes the underlying situation worse.[12]

Slow Down

Talking slowly gives your mind time to catch up with your emotions and is a simple but powerful way to prevent damage from hasty words. As we've discussed, feeling breathless (breathing heavily after talking) or feeling like a conversation is racing ahead of you is usually a warning sign that the Neanderthal is in the driver's seat and the conversation is in danger of escalating (or has already escalated). Slowing down allows restraint to elbow its way back into an interaction and to safeguard the underlying relationship from impulsive and harmful words.

Lose the Length

There really is such a thing as "too much information," especially in emotionally charged conversations. Our interpersonal bandwidth fills up quickly when discussing sensitive issues, so instead of making three points during a two-minute monologue, make one point slowly and clearly in a minute or less. You can offer other points, if necessary, during your subsequent conversational turns. It's easy to mentally overload your conversational partner if you subject her to a barrage of emotionally laden words or points. She may also get hung up on a single issue (out of three that you raised) and not process anything else. Short responses make it easier for people to follow a discussion and increase the likelihood that productive dialogue can emerge.

Orient to the Context

As I tell clients (and remind myself) all the time, your conversations aren't simulations: this is your *actual* life, and your words are actively shaping your present and your future. So look around the room before you talk and consider the implications of your words. That's not your fake boss, your hologram kids, or your imaginary colleague you're about to unload on. All your conversations are real. Communicate with this in mind.

Welcome a Response

We-based interpersonal communication takes two people. It's just I-based talk until you include the other person. And there is almost always another side to a sensitive issue, so listen to what your partner is saying and update your thinking to include his perspective.

Go slowly when you are in an identity-related conversation or when you need to have a sensitive discussion of any kind. Slow conversations are almost always civilized and civilized conversations—characterized by mutual restraint and containment—are *always* safe because they don't cause relational damage. As long as your conversation remains civilized, you can talk about anything.

Whether you *should* talk about something, however, is a question that often deserves thoughtful consideration. Sometimes, no conversation is a great conversational choice.

And at other times, a boring, but civilized, conversation is exactly what you need.

15

BE BORING

MOST CONVERSATIONS ARE EXCITING FOR ALL THE WRONG REASONS

On a typically sunny Los Angeles afternoon, I took a stroll around the neighborhood with Felix, my one-year-old nephew who, even by southern California standards, has a laid-back, easygoing disposition. (I sometimes call him Little Dude, after Jeff Bridges's character in *The Big Lebowski*.)

Felix and I returned from our long walk to find my four-year-old niece, full of vigor and creativity (and probably missing the center stage), waiting by the door and making loud monster noises. This must have either scared Felix or grated on his nerves, because he let loose with an atypical bout of wailing.

The crying brought in the cavalry. My sister and brother-in-law, also known as Mom and Dad in this house, rushed in and began to argue about the cause of Felix's crying—loud noise or hunger? By now my niece had entered the racket with some wailing of her own, and when the blame for Felix's crying landed on me, I seriously considered joining her. I had overextended our walk and messed up his feeding time, my sister informed me. Unable to squirm out of the verdict, I meekly apologized and handed over my nephew.

A few minutes later, peace had been restored. A well-fed Felix went down serenely for a nap. My sister and brother-in-law went outside to do some yard work, and my niece went with them. I took advantage of the calm to make some tea. When I started to follow everyone outside, I stopped in the doorway, struck by what I saw.

While my niece was happily playing in the sandbox, her parents were taking advantage of the moment to talk. They were leaning in closely and communicating in the way that people sometimes do when they feel as if they are the only two people in the whole world.

I turned around and left them alone.

Less than 30 minutes after outright household pandemonium, these two were huddled together, having a conversation so engrossing that I dared not interrupt. That's real life, and that's real communication.

It's tempting to romanticize communication and mistakenly assume that the best conversations are also the most exciting ones. Conversations can be exciting for a variety of reasons: they are intense or high stakes, they bring big news, they are filled with emotions, or they contain something unexpected or novel. But exciting conversations are relatively rare and don't always go our way. In reality, good, meaningful communication often looks plain, unremarkable, and boring.

Some of our most important and most cherished moments of connection occur without fanfare, interspersed throughout our daily lives. These moments happen frequently because of the inherently social nature of humans, but they are seldom flashy or exciting. The danger is that we overlook these meaningful but commonplace moments because we are anticipating more exhilarating and stimulating interactions.

Drawn to Excitement, Led to Failure

Excitement is the temptress of the digital age. Left behind—widely derided and profoundly unappreciated—is the temptress's frumpy and dull stepsister of routine, simple, and unadorned communication.

It's hard for many of us to imagine something more out of step with the digital era than anything boring. Excitement, novelty, and intensity are wired into the digital age. Showy new devices hit the market constantly. Companies compete to get their sleek, attractive digital communication tools into customers' hands, rolling their products out at splashy, attention-grabbing events. CEOs of tech companies are treated like celebrities, and the best devices and apps are referred to as cool, hip, and sexy.

That expectation of excitement has crept into our interpersonal communication. We mistakenly embrace the notion that communication should be as flashy, stimulating, and entertaining as the sleek devices that facilitate it. Our interactions should bring something new and improved to the relationship; a situation should resolve itself with a clever line and a witty summary; laughter and inspiration should accompany our text messages; and great news should fill our inboxes. But expecting our communication to be consistently exciting is unrealistic and unsustainable. Exciting, high-intensity conversations are notoriously failure prone.

Exciting conversations frequently fail because high emotional intensity signals our inner Neanderthal that something's going on, and this puts our quick-acting, club-swinging instincts on high alert. Consequently, escalation happens faster and is more severe during high-intensity conversations.

It also takes an enormous amount of energy to maintain an intense conversation. Think back to interactions that have left you physically drained, like an emergency discussion about a serious work problem, an argument with a colleague, or a critical sales meeting. Those high-intensity conversations consumed a great deal of energy and probably required you to take a recovery break afterward. Most people can't—and shouldn't—maintain high-intensity conversations for long periods of time, because as the cognitive load of the discussion saps our energy and depletes our willpower, our restraint is weakened and damaging words are more likely to slip out.[1]

On the other hand, routine interpersonal communication is sustainable day after day. We build bonds with our coworkers and clients as we work through regular processes and issues; we develop trust with our bosses over a series of mostly unremarkable interactions; and we build our families, marriages, and friendships in the regular interactions that, over time, shape, sustain, and strengthen our relationships.

It's not really excitement and intensity that we want from our conversations; we want bosses, coworkers, family, and friends we can count on. And they want the same from us. Relationships are built through thousands of routine and unremarkable interactions. That's how people come to trust us and see that we're consistent. Boring is dependable. Bland is steady. Over time, what seems unremarkable turns out to be quite remarkable after all.

Hold That Thought

Not long ago I was facilitating a conference call between Jim and Sarah, who were negotiating an amicable divorce agreement. The call was boring but efficient, until the end. They had resolved most of the major financial and custody issues, and we were close to finalizing the whole agreement when Sarah unexpectedly became upset at Jim's recommendation for splitting the carpooling duties. Before I could do anything to stop it, Sarah lambasted Jim for being "selfish, controlling, and pathetic." And for good measure she added that he was going to end up "broken-down and lonely, just like his father."

The conversation was no longer boring. I could hear Jim gather his breath for what I assumed to be an equally potent response. Additional damage was imminent, so I jumped in and told Jim that I needed to talk to Sarah alone and that I'd follow up with him later.

After Jim hung up, Sarah and I talked for a while, and she agreed to apologize for her outburst. The three of us ultimately finalized the agreement, but Jim was never the same on our future calls. After that, Jim was silent for long periods of time, he contributed very little, and he focused all his energy on getting off the phone at the earliest opportunity. Sarah's criticism was like the single grain of sand that finally shifted the whole pile. Her harsh outburst changed something in their relationship. No doubt they were having trouble before—they were getting a divorce, after all—but Sarah's pointed criticism demonstrated how easily thoughtless communication can make a bad situation worse. Don't make the mistake of thinking that a dismal relationship can't deteriorate further. A worse relationship is only one hasty sentence away.

When I'm consulting with clients in conflict, I advise them to keep their conversations as bland as possible. Boring conversations reduce the chance of relational damage, because negative emotions lurk around every corner in a conflict. Boring conversations allow people to interact in a subdued way that minimizes unnecessary drama and protects the underlying relationship against further damage.

When there's a great deal of negative emotional energy just beneath the surface (like there is in most conflicts), it's not a good idea to unnecessarily put feelings into words. People often find it difficult to express feelings because emotions aren't always straightforward (*Am I angry or just frustrated? Is something else making me feel this way? Am I overreacting? Am I underreacting?*) and because emotions can change frequently, even within a single interaction. Don't force anyone, including yourself, to convert *unspoken* confusion and uncertainty into *actual* confusion and uncertainty by feeling that you need to vocalize everything you're feeling in a conflict-laden conversation. Spare, boring conversations reduce the chance for harm.

Research suggests that conflict-laden interactions are especially problematic when one or both parties are under outside stress.[2] Many of your most damaging interactions probably happened when you were wrestling with something else, and all of a sudden an unexpected conversation was dropped into your lap. So if you are experiencing chronic or acute stress caused by, say, illness, caregiving, or a period of job or relational uncertainty—or if you know that your conversational partner is in a similarly stressful situation—tread lightly, and remember that a high-intensity conversation carries additional dangers in these cases.

All relationships—even our strongest ones—are sensitive to words, and when a conversation escalates, damaging words are more likely to come out. The principle of asymmetry bears repeating here: connections can only be built slowly, one solid, dependable, and usually boring interaction at a time. But we can dismantle these relationships in a single exciting conversation. That's communication's asymmetry. And when we take our relationships apart, like Humpty Dumpty, they might not go back together again.

Communication has consequences.

The Last Straw

Intense or exciting conversations fail momentously if they lead to the moment when one person decides that he has finally had enough. In the example of Jim and Sarah, Jim had the option to (further) withdraw from the tarnished relationship following Sarah's outburst. Most of us can't withdraw from or discontinue work relationships as easily, so deformed relationships must often limp along, sowing discontent and tension for months or years.

Whether or not you can walk away, the "that's it" moment fundamentally changes the underlying relationship. There's nothing in this book, and no amount of counseling or consulting, that can unwind that moment once it happens. Two people move from one relationship (before) to another (after), and the two relationships are not the same. In this case, the best I can do as a consultant is help the parties become familiar with the reality of the altered relationship.

Relational transformations like this are unintentional consequences of intense conversations, which is another reason not to wander around itching to bring some excitement into your everyday communication.

It's impossible to know when and if a particular conversation might trigger a "that's it" moment that permanently alters a relationship, but if you're already feeling tension with a coworker or if your boss is already under pressure about slow revenue growth, an exciting, intense conversation is the last thing you want. Boring and low-key conversations will allow you to conduct the business you need to do while minimizing the likelihood of a transformative relational event.

There's no need to run away from a high-intensity conversation if it happens—by this point in the book, you have all the tools you need to handle *important* high-intensity conversations. But to modify some advice from the last chapter, just because you can handle an exciting conversation doesn't mean that you should race out and start one.

Excitement Addicts

Maintaining a bland, low-intensity conversation is easier for some people than others. There are three types of people you'll probably encounter at some point—possibly tomorrow—who are addicted to exciting conversations. *Drama kings and queens* make every conversation a production and turn even the smallest of issues into major problems. *Prima donnas* have a voracious appetite for attention. And *hyperactives* have way too much energy and are hard to handle because they bounce around erratically in a conversation.

Drama royals, prima donnas, and hyperactives can make enormous demands on your time and on your conversational energy. If you find yourself in regular contact with these excitement addicts, four tips can help you stabilize your conversations:

1. **Stop talking.** Excitable people want to talk, want attention, or both, so give them some space to have their say. This is going to happen anyway, so don't fight it. It's the path of least resistance, and they might even relax some after they talk.

2. **Keep the intensity low when you do talk.** Use your conversational turns to drive down the intensity of the interaction. Your understated responses can often reduce some of the drama in the conversation.

3. **Redirect to the main point in strategic conversations.** Conversations with excitement addicts often bounce from point to point. This usually isn't a problem in a nonstrategic conversation where there's no objective; but in a goal-directed (strategic) conversation, this lack of focus is often debilitating. When the conversation matters, avoid tangents and redirect back to the root issue to keep your goal in play.

4. **Don't bring any unnecessary drama to the conversation.** The last thing a conversation with an excitable person needs is more excitement. Don't add additional emotional material to the discussion, and be wary of adding anything substantive. Stick to one modest goal (whatever you are trying to accomplish) in strategic conversations. In nonstrategic conversations, let the person talk himself out.

High-intensity people play a dangerous game that they often lose. It's usually only a matter of time until prima donnas and drama kings and queens initiate a high-intensity conversation at the wrong time (hyperactives are usually perceived less malevolently). Because their flamboyant and self-centered style makes continuous withdrawals from their interpersonal goodwill accounts, prima donnas and drama royals often get bounced out of their jobs and relationships, with few people sorry to see them go by the time of their final flameout.

Despite the contemporary perception that exciting communication is successful communication, it destroys many more relationships than it builds or improves. Competent, routine, and unremarkable communication leads to meaningful interactions, which, one after another, improve our overall quality of life.

All those boring interactions add up. Over time, that's how we build relationships that are worth getting excited about.

Now it's time to discuss something that we've been cheering about forever. Gather around—it's story time.

16

GIVE PEOPLE WHAT THEY WANT

FEW THINGS CONNECT LIKE A STORY

Not long ago I gathered with my mother's family to celebrate a seventieth birthday. With all her siblings present, the stories poured out one after the other. I begged my uncle to tell me again about the time that he and my granddad were trimming a backyard tree, and he obliged. The story goes like this:

> Years ago my uncle and his dad (my granddad) decided it was time to prune back some limbs that were growing too close to the house. My granddad, who was 80 years old at the time, climbed a tall ladder that he had leaned against a sturdy limb and began trimming with a handsaw. My uncle was collecting the limbs as they fell when all of a sudden the ladder, the saw, a large limb, and my granddad came crashing to the potato patch below. My granddad had mistakenly sawed off the limb that the ladder was resting on.
>
> "Dad, are you all right?" my uncle asked frantically.

"No, I'm not all right," my granddad replied in his Newfoundland brogue, "I ruined me potatoes, me poor potatoes."

Around the table, everyone laughed. Then my uncle paused a moment, and said, "I know how much you all love Dad, and he knows it too. He's been lonely since Mom died, but all of your calls and visits have really helped. I'm so grateful. Thank you."

It was an accident that my granddad sawed off the wrong limb and fell into his potatoes, but it's no accident that a story triggered a strong sense of connection. The images and memories brought up by the story opened up a window for sharing that my uncle climbed through. A simple story led to a meaningful moment of connection.

Storytelling—the final part of your communicator's toolkit—is a powerful higher-order communication skill that grabs attention and can bring people together. Unfortunately, our verbal storytelling skills are in peril from twin threats, just when it's harder than ever to get people's attention.

Verbal Story Time Is in Danger

On one hand, verbal storytelling is being elbowed aside by stripped-down messages, information, and data. The tendency in the digital age to cut messages down to their most expedient form sacrifices richer context for pared-down information. It's faster for me to say that Sarah's a good colleague than it is to tell you about the time she pulled an all-nighter helping me get ready for a client presentation. It's quicker for me to tell you what I want than it is for me to explain what I want, why I want it, and how that relates to you.

But in communication, as we've seen, what's fast and expedient for me often comes at the cost of your understanding. You'll know more about Sarah (and about me) if I take the time to paint the picture instead of just giving you the data. That's the difference between *showing* and *telling*, between *communicating* and just *talking*.

At the same time, verbal storytelling is also increasingly marginalized as the "old" way of telling a story—face-to-face—has faded, and mediated storytelling through video and image-sharing sites has exploded.

There have never been more ways to digitally tell our stories. We can blog, shoot a video and upload it to Facebook or YouTube, or tell a story through images on social media sites. And we do these things in staggering numbers—over a billion people on Facebook and 72 hours of video uploaded every minute on YouTube—which highlights our propensity as a storytelling, connecting species.[1] The proliferation of devices that record images and platforms that share stories are two very noteworthy facets of the communication revolution. Our devices have changed the ways we connect, share, and remember things, and they have even—when used in popular uprisings like the Arab Spring—changed the course of history.

We shouldn't turn our back on *any* communication innovation that allows us to connect and share with others. But let's not entirely displace our oral storytelling tradition with YouTube videos and Pinterest accounts on one side and abbreviated e-mails and text messages on the other.

Verbal storytelling is a descriptive, higher-order communication skill, and as such it is prone to degradation from lack of use. I'm not worried that my niece and nephew won't know how to tell a digital story. They were born into the hyperconnected era, and they are remarkably adept at navigating all things digital. I am, however, concerned that they might not have the same exposure to verbal storytelling that I did growing up in the decades before the digital communication revolution.

The same teenager who can shoot, edit, and post a short film in a matter of hours also needs to be able to tell his best friend about his weekend. It's nice that people can get a sense for how much I love Hawaii by looking at my photos online, but I should also be able to communicate how Hawaii makes me feel through verbal stories of my time there. In a job interview, a prospective employee needs to be able to offer relevant and compelling narrative accounts of past achievements, not just hand the interviewer a current résumé. And employees need more than facts alone to be reassured that the sweeping structural changes you are recommending are worth implementing; they need to understand the grand narrative of the initiative.

A couple years ago, I was chatting with my six-year-old niece, Iris, via Skype, and I could see she was rapidly losing interest in our conversation. My questions about her day were met with flat, one-word answers. She started to fidget, looking to her mother for permission to end the conversation. Knowing that I was losing her attention, I reached into my toolkit and pulled out old faithful—a story.

I improvised a tale about going to see a doctor because my leg hurt. I gave vivid details about the pain, and I told Iris about the eccentric doctor who treated me (he dressed in a top hat and started all his sentences by saying "My good man"). After examining my leg thoroughly, he pulled out a pad, wrote a prescription, and handed it over to me. I was surprised to see that only two words were written on the prescription: *ice cream.*

"Why'd he write 'ice cream' on the prescription?" Iris asked.

"That's precisely what I asked the doctor," I replied, and then paused.

"Well? What'd he say?" she pressed.

I replied that the doctor said, "My good man, ice cream is good for you!"

Iris burst out laughing. The line "ice cream is good for you" would become something that we'd repeat to each other for months. Our faltering conversation was rescued by the irresistible lure of a story.

My niece didn't love the story because it was *about* ice cream; she loved it because it *was* ice cream. Storytelling is like conversational dessert that we can have at any time.

What's So Great About Stories

Stories Are Irresistible

Think about how you loved stories as a child and how you begged your parents to read you one more at bedtime. Do you remember how story time was the best part of elementary school (next to recess)?

Stories aren't just an entertaining part of our childhood; they're an inextricable part of our shared human history. Long before texts and tweets, and even before paper and parchment, we told stories to communicate. That's our heritage.

Stories have survived as a way of passing along knowledge, in part, because they are powerful explanatory tools. Stories generate more interest than "straight" information, and we understand and remember information better when it is presented in narrative form with a clear ending.[2] Stories also activate our minds, which increases our conversational engagement.[3] And stories simplify abstract or complex matters into something more comprehensible.[4] Put these strengths together, and you have a lesson that you learned in kindergarten: people love stories.

I use narrative (stories) all the time in my consulting, especially in organizational change initiatives where uncertainty abounds and people are trying to get their minds around what's happening. The story of a company transitioning from childhood to adolescence, for example, helps people understand more clearly why their organization is experiencing growing pains. A narrative that traces a company's history from an idea on the back of a napkin, to a parent's basement, to an office tower is far more likely to stick in employees' minds and help establish the context than a list of dates and milestones.

If I tell you that my company values keeping our educational content up to date, you *hear* what I'm saying. If I tell you about the time I updated my presentation in the parking lot 30 minutes before I was due on stage because I'd just heard about a new study on the radio, you *see* what I'm saying. People love (and remember) vivid stories, examples, illustrations, and other descriptions of people, places, things, and ideas.[5]

Watch what happens when stories emerge in your conversations. People *can't help* but pay attention. Stories cut through the fog of distraction and grab people's interest. In the digital age, where it's easy to send a message, but hard to get anyone to notice, storytelling is an indispensable communication skill.

Stories Convey Information the Way We Want to Hear It

A motorcycle policeman once crashed into a car I was driving.

I'll explain this true incident later, but notice what's already happened: you probably "see" parts of the story in your mind, and you've started forming your own narrative. *It was raining. It was sunny. It was day. It was night. I was alone. People were with me. It was on the highway. It was on a city street. It was on a country road. The policeman was on a Harley. He was on a Honda. It was Geoff's fault. It was the lawman's fault.* After only one sentence, your mental storytelling was already off and running.

Stories are so intricately woven into the human fabric that we have a predisposition toward creating them, even when all we have are the barest of details.[6] Give humans some information, and we'll put it together and create a story. We do this all the time. If I notice that Jim doesn't feel like talking this morning, I'll take that information, add it to a conversation we had earlier about marriage trouble, and develop a story that he had an argument with his wife. If the boss starts treating me differently, I'll stay up at night creating stories about what might be happening. If I lose a customer, I form a story to explain why (and probably hang some of the blame on an external excuse to let myself off lightly). If I get a new client, I create a story that highlights what a great salesman I am (making an internal attribution for the success to give myself full credit).

We translate the information we receive about our world and the people in it into story form to make sense of our surroundings. When we communicate with stories, there is less chance of slippage between what we say and what someone hears because people are converting information into stories continuously. Stories are already in the "language" we prefer.

Stories Provide a Safer Way to Talk

For centuries, teachers have used fables, parables, and other stories to provide a safer way to communicate about touchy topics. Stories can minimize a listener's reflexive resistance to what we're saying and can encourage people to draw their own conclusions.

Back to the police officer who crashed into me.

I was turning left into a cemetery as part of a funeral procession when a motorcycle policeman patrolling the line crashed into my driver's side door. Right after I felt the impact and saw the officer lying on the ground, I jumped out of the car to see if he was hurt. Thankfully, he was a little disoriented but otherwise fine. I helped him up, and we determined that although his motorcycle was largely spared from damage, my driver's side door had a big dent in it.

Complicating matters, the police officer's uniform indicated that he was a master accident inspector—that's what he did for a living—and his initial comments suggested that he might be looking for a way to pin blame for the accident on me.

I ignored his initial comments (using the 60-second rule) and told him how glad I was that he wasn't hurt. It took a few moments of nonthreatening discussion and some space for the police officer to self-correct, but he eventually took the blame for the accident (he was driving down the center line of the road without his siren on and hit my door while I was turning left; only by driving sideways could I have hit him in this scenario).

Once he admitted that he was at fault, I told him that it was up to him whether or not we called for an accident report. I didn't imagine that it would be good for a master accident investigator to call in an investigation of himself, so I gave him that choice. All I wanted was to get my dented door fixed. He chose to skip the report, and he paid out of his pocket for the repairs.

Every time I tell this story, it generates a type of discussion that I'd normally be reluctant to wander directly into. It exposes several sensitive, identity-related topics: law and authority, ethical decision making, and responses to stress. Such topics can easily provoke sharp responses, but stories can protect conversations by providing a less threatening way to talk about core beliefs and deeply felt opinions. Some people think I should have forced the policeman to call in the accident for an official police report. Others would have been willing to pay for the door on their own and not force the officer to pay. Some people get mad at the officer for initially blaming me for the wreck.

By talking about how they might have handled the situation differently, people express their beliefs just as clearly as though it was a simple statement of fact. But by communicating *through* my story, the ground is safer for people to talk about issues that might otherwise be too hot to handle.

Stories are peerless communication tools. They grab people's attention, help people understand, are more easily remembered, and provide a safer way to talk about sensitive issues. But stories also perform one more vital function.

Stories Draw Us Closer Together

My friend Bill was fighting cancer, and I took him to several of his medical appointments when he was too sick or fatigued to drive. At one early chemotherapy treatment, Bill explained that he was having difficulty finding an effective antinausea medication. The first two drugs he tried hadn't worked, so his oncologist prescribed a new one. I immediately asked if there was a *fourth* pill we could try, in case the third one failed. Both my friend and his oncologist were puzzled, so I explained with a story.

When I went through the army's Ranger School, it was winter. The Ranger instructors (RIs) called cold-weather gear like gloves, wool hats, and face covers "snivel gear," since we weak and sniveling Ranger students were not tough enough, according to the RIs, to handle the elements.

Naturally, it took a blizzard before the RIs would let us put on any snivel gear. But even when we were allowed the luxury, there was an ironclad rule among us: no matter how cold it was, *you never put on your last piece of snivel gear.* One piece was always left unused in your rucksack, because once it was gone, your situation could never improve. And this would be a devastating mental blow to a freezing Ranger student.

The doctor understood right away. "So you want to make sure that the third prescription isn't the last piece of snivel gear?"

"You got it, Ranger," I said. With months of chemotherapy remaining, I didn't want to contemplate that my friend's nausea might not improve.

The snivel gear story helped the oncologist understand my fears. It also struck a chord with him, because he had been concerned for some time that his patients didn't fully appreciate how many different options were available for chemotherapy-related nausea. He asked if he could share the story with his patients as a way of encouraging them to speak up if their medications weren't working (I readily agreed).

Bill eventually found a drug that eliminated most of his nausea, and throughout the process the oncologist—a good sport—eased our minds by repeatedly telling us that we were never going to run out of snivel gear. Sharing that story helped me, my friend, and his oncologist draw a bit closer together, in a way that hours of previous appointments and checkups never did.

The robust power of stories explains why I can send you 10 informational e-mails and we still might feel like strangers, but after we share only one or two stories, we often seem more like friends. And it's okay that a story might only draw us slightly closer together, because *slightly* and *slowly* are how we build strong, enduring relationships.

Stories don't have to be perfect, brilliant, or even very long. Ministories like nicknames and metaphors can help paint a quick verbal picture and draw people in to what you're saying.[7] Your stories (and ministories) don't need to be flawlessly scripted. Stories that make a point without rambling and, when possible, involve some sharing are all that you need to harness the power of narrative.

While personal stories are often most effective, don't hesitate to use secondhand stories, anecdotes, and examples to make your point. If you hear or read a good story on the Internet, on the radio, at work, or wherever, make a note of it and consider how you might use it. Think like a storyteller, gathering stories and looking for opportunities to spread them.

Sharing stories draws people together and facilitates meaningful connections. And thinking like a storyteller shouldn't be too much of a stretch for you anyway. After all, it runs in our human family.

Storyteller Ron Evans tells about an African village without electricity where people would gather in the evenings and listen to tales from the griot (storyteller).[8] When electricity finally came to the village, the tribe bought a television and abandoned the griot to watch TV. But after a few weeks, people started returning to hear the griot once again.

An anthropologist studying the village witnessed this turn of events and asked a villager, "Why do you return to the griot? After all, the television knows many stories and never gets tired."

The villager replied: "The television knows many stories, but the griot knows me."

Connection: The Happy Ending to the Digital Communication Revolution

Successful communication in the digital age requires higher- and lower-order communication. It will take effort to maintain our higher-order communication skills in a predominately lower-order environment, but if we allow our higher-order skills to atrophy, the productive and meaningful communication we want will too often elude us.

Let's embrace new ways to connect while also retaining the timeless ability to tell stories that don't involve turning on a computer. Let's introduce ourselves to a new acquaintance without referring someone to our social media page, troubleshoot an interpersonal issue face-to-face instead of through a dozen e-mails, tell a client or boss what we mean without reading from our slides, express heartfelt birthday wishes instead of resorting to a preset Facebook message, and comfort our friends in real time when they need it the most. These higher-order communication skills aren't outdated; they're eternal.

No matter how many new devices flood the market, no matter how powerful our computers get, and no matter how automated our environment becomes, our work and our personal lives will always have one constant: people.

We can't afford to lose our capacity to share things that aren't measured in bytes, to connect slowly and without devices, to reconcile feuding coworkers as well as spreadsheets, to look into eyes as well as at screens, and to not just "like" people, but to *actually* like them.

Connectivity is no guarantee of connection, and connection is what we're really after. The ability to connect with another person is one of the simplest and most powerfully resonant pleasures of life. It's also the most effective way to get things done. As the griot story shows, personal connections give our life meaning in irreplaceable ways and create enduring bonds at work, in families, in communities, and in our world.

Our primordial urge to connect and our love of communication will pull us onward to our next conversation, and the one after that, and the one after that. It's up to us to retain the higher-order communication skills we need to make the interactions count.

Good communication = good relationships = good life, at work and at home (and on the moon if humans ever move there). The ways that we communicate—and the ways that we don't—shape our relationships, and our relationships shape our lives. The most important people in our lives deserve our very best communication.

Two people talking, without devices, distractions, or anything else coming in between, is a vital and cherished part of our past that we need to safeguard for the future.

Your future begins with your next conversation.

Here's to the life of your higher-order dreams, built one conversation at a time.

NOTES

INTRODUCTION

1   My thoughts about the transportation revolution versus the communication revolution were inspired by Matt Ridley, *The Rational Optimist: How Prosperity Evolves* (New York: HarperCollins, 2010), p. 354. My thinking was extended by Dan Ariely, *The Upside of Irrationality: The Unexpected Benefits of Defying Logic at Work and at Home* (New York: HarperCollins, 2010), pp. 7–9. Please note that communication includes verbal and written (or typed) modalities throughout the book unless otherwise specified.

2   Edward Tenner, *Why Things Bite Back* (New York: Vintage Books, 1996), p. 186.

3   Theo Emery, "In Tennessee, Goats Eat the 'Vine That Ate the South,'" *New York Times*, June 5, 2007, http://www.nytimes.com/2007/06/05/us/05goats.html.

4   Recent books marshaling evidence of collateral damage from the digital revolution include Jaron Lanier, *Who Owns the Future?* (New York, Simon & Schuster, 2013); Larry Rosen, *iDisorder: Understanding Our Obsession with Technology and Overcoming Its Hold on Us* (New York: Palgrave Macmillan, 2012); Clay A. Anderson, *The Information Diet: A Case for Conscious Consumption* (Sebastopol, CA: O'Reilly: 2012); Elias Aboujaoude, *Virtually You: The Dangerous Powers of the e-Personality* (New York: W. W. Norton, 2011); Jaron Lanier, *You Are Not a Gadget: A Manifesto* (New York: Alfred A. Knopf, 2010); and Nicholas Carr, *The Shallows: What the Internet Is Doing to Our Brains* (New York: W. W. Norton, 2010). Earlier books that sounded the alarm include Sherry Turkle, *Life on the Screen: Identity in the Age of the Internet* (New York: Touchstone, 1997); John L. Locke, *The De-Voicing of Society: Why We Don't Talk to Each Other Anymore* (New York: Simon & Schuster, 1998); and Patricia Wallace, *The Psychology of the Internet* (Cambridge: Cambridge University Press, 1999). Other books on this topic appear in the Recommended Reading.

5   Unless otherwise specified (e.g. phone conversation, face-to-face conversation, e-mail conversation), conversations are defined expansively to include verbal and written (or typed) communication.

6   See J. Gregory Trafton and Christopher A. Monk, "Task Interruptions," in *Reviews of Human Factors and Ergonomics*, ed. Deborah A. Boehm-Davis (Santa Monica, CA: Human Factors and Ergonomics Society), vol. 3, chap. 4; and Maggie Jackson, *Distracted: The Erosion of Attention and the Coming Dark Age* (Amherst, NY: Prometheus Books, 2008), pp. 11–26. Additional sources appear in the Recommended Reading.

7   Roy F. Baumeister and John Tierney, *Willpower: Rediscovering the Greatest Human Strength* (New York: Penguin, 2011), pp. 35–60.

8   See Damian Thompson, *The Fix: How Addiction Is Invading Our Lives and Taking Over Your World* (London: Collins, 2012), pp. 1–24; and Daniel Akst, *We Have Met the Enemy* (New York: Penguin, 2011), pp. 153–154.

9   An early version of my thoughts about quick, cheap, and easy communication appeared on my blog at http://mouthpeaceconsulting. com on January 6, 2012. I started blogging weekly while writing *Stop Talking, Start Communicating*, and some of the ideas in this book first debuted on my blog. I've noted throughout the book where significant portions of my blog entries appear in the book.

10 Perspective taking is included in our definition of interpersonal communication to highlight that it's not just the number of people you are talking to that demarcates personal, interpersonal, and mass communication. How you talk to your conversational partner, (e.g., I-based or we-based), is also a factor.

11 George Eliot, *Felix Holt, the Radical* (Buki Editions, 2009), Kindle edition, chap. 29.

12 Pamela Paul, "Don't Call Me, I Won't Call You," *New York Times*, March 18, 2011, http://www.nytimes.com/2011/03/20/ fashion/20Cultural.html. See also Sherry Turkle, *Alone Together: Why We Expect More from Technology and Less from Each Other* (New York: Basic Books, 2011), pp. 203–209.

13 Barbara L. Fredrickson, *Love 2.0: How Our Supreme Emotion Affects Everything We Feel, Think, Do, and Become* (New York: Hudson Street, 2013), p. 54 and Barbara L. Fredrickson, "Your Phone vs. Your Heart," *New York Times*, March 23, 2013, http://www.nytimes. com/2013/03/24/opinion/sunday/your-phone-vs-your-heart.html.

CHAPTER I

1   Information about Ian Rowland and cold reading comes from Ian Rowland, *The Full Facts of Cold Reading*, 4th ed. (London: Ian Rowland Limited, 2005), pp. 134–155.

2   With the exception of Bernie in the next story, my niece, Iris, and my nephew, Felix, names of people, identifying information about companies, and minor details in examples have been changed throughout the book to maintain confidentiality.

3   For example, see Teresa M. Amabile and Steven J. Kramer, *The Progress Principle: Using Small Wins to Ignite Joy, Engagement, and Creativity at Work* (Boston, MA: Harvard Business Review Press, 2011), Kindle edition, chap. 7 and Barbara L. Fredrickson, *Love 2.0: How Our Supreme Emotion Affects Everything We Feel, Think, Do, and Become* (New York: Hudson Street, 2013), pp. 20–27.

4   Part of the disharmony was due to a company structure that hadn't kept pace with the organization's success, resulting in a work environment that was confusing for employees ("Who's supposed to be doing the new work? I thought that was my job."). This ambiguity generated interpersonal conflict ("Why didn't this get done? Why are you doing my job?") and required us to modify the company structure to reduce the task and role confusion. The restructuring eliminated many of the relational conflict issues, and the interpersonal conflicts that remained—where the problems *really were* about the people—stood out like sore thumbs and were quickly handled with frank conversations. We talk more about the role of structure on communication in Chapter 13.

CHAPTER 2

1   I'm not the first person to use this phrase with respect to the digital revolution. A slight variation of it appears as the subtitle in Sherry Turkle's *Alone Together: Why We Expect More from Technology and Less from Each Other* (New York: Basic Books, 2011).

2   Schumpeter, "Slaves to the Smartphone," *Economist*, March 10, 2012, http://www.economist.com/node/21549904.

3   Maggie Jackson, *Distracted: The Erosion of Attention and the Coming Dark Age* (Amherst, New York: Prometheus Books, 2008), pp. 75–86.

4   You can get a glimpse of how fragmented our communication preferences have become by observing how you receive messages on your birthday. Birthday greetings will come to you from every conceivable communication channel.

5   Yelling breaches the protective blanket of civility that safeguards most interactions. Furthermore, verbally aggressive behaviors reduce the (immediate) cognitive abilities of the recipient; see Anat Rafaeli et al, "When Customers Exhibit Verbal Aggression, Employees Pay

Cognitive Costs," *Journal of Applied Psychology*, vol. 97, no. 5 (September 2012), pp. 944–945, doi: 10.1037/a0028559.

6   For a general discussion of how leader behaviors impact organizational culture, see Edgar H. Schein, *Organizational Culture and Leadership*, 2nd ed. (San Francisco: Jossey-Bass, 1992), pp. 228–253.

7   Robert B. Cialdini, *Influence: Science and Practice*, 4th ed. (Boston: Allyn and Bacon, 2001), pp. 100–111.

8   Mark L. Knapp and Anita L. Vangelisti, *Interpersonal Communication and Human Relationships*, 4th ed. (Boston: Allyn and Bacon, 2000), pp. 12–13.

9   John Medina, *Brain Rules: Twelve Principles for Surviving and Thriving at Work, Home, and School* (Seattle, WA: Pear Press, 2008), pp. 269–270. See also Kelly McGonigal, *The Willpower Instinct: How Self-Control Works, Why It Matters, and What You Can Do About It* (New York: Avery, 2012), pp. 187–188.

10   Robert Rosenthal and Lenore Jacobson, *Pygmalion in the Classroom: Teacher Expectation and Pupils' Intellectual Development* (New York: Holt, Rinehart, and Winston, 1968), pp. 65–66.

11   Ibid., p. 70.

12   Ibid., pp. 98–108.

13   Rosenthal and Jacobson's experiment is discussed in detail in *Pygmalion in the Classroom*, pp. 61–120. The methodology used by Rosenthal and Jacobson has received some scholarly criticism; see, for example, Augustine Brannigan, *The Rise and Fall of Social Psychology: The Use and Misuse of the Experimental Method, Social Problems and Social Issues* (Hawthorne, NY: Aldine de Gruyter, 2004), pp. 74–90. However, a meta-analysis supports the existence of Pygmalion effects: D. Brian McNatt, "Ancient Pygmalion Joins Contemporary Management: A Meta-Analysis of the Result," *Journal of Applied Psychology*, vol. 85, no. 2 (2000), pp. 318–320, doi:10.1037/0021-9010.85.2.314.

CHAPTER 3

1   Stephen R. Covey, *The 7 Habits of Highly Effective People* (New York: Free Press, 2004; first published in 1989 by Simon & Schuster), p. 101. Covey's story uses workers and managers as characters.

2   George E. Vaillant, *Triumphs of Experience: The Men of the Harvard Grant Study* (Cambridge, MA: Belknap Press, 2012), p. 54; see also George E. Vaillant, *Aging Well: Surprising Guideposts to a Happier Life from the Landmark Harvard Study of Adult Development* (Boston: Little, Brown, 2002), pp. 16–21.

3   Vaillant, *Triumphs of Experience*, pp. 393–394, 398–410.

4   Joshua Wolf Shenk, "What Makes Us Happy," *The Atlantic*, June 2009, http://www.theatlantic.com/magazine/archive/2009/06/what-makes-us-happy/307439. The quoted passage is located on the third page online. Vaillant stood by this claim in his most recent book; see Vaillant, *Triumphs of Experience*, pp. 191–192.

CHAPTER 4

1   Peninnah Schram, *Ten Classic Jewish Children's Stories* (New York: Pitspopany, 1998), pp. 40–41. Permission granted by Peninnah Schram, copyright holder, to use this slightly modified version of a midrashic story, which comes from several Jewish sources, including Proverbs 18:21 and Psalms 39:2. *Author's note:* This story contains verbatim sentences from Peninnah Schram's work. The story, as it appears, is most appropriately considered as Schram's story, which I have slightly modified, and which she has graciously given permission to use.

2   James Boswell, *The Life of Samuel Johnson, L.L.D.* (London: John Sharpe, 1830), p. 367, http://books.google.com/books?id=2d0-AAAAYAAJ.

3   Marcial Losada and Emily Heaphy, "The Role of Positivity and Connectivity in the Performance of Business Teams: A Nonlinear Dynamics Model," *American Behavioral Scientist*, vol. 47, no. 6 (2004), pp. 740–765, doi: 10.1177/0002764203260208; and John M. Gottman, *What Predicts Divorce: The Relationship Between Marital Processes and Marital Outcomes* (Hillsdale, NJ: Lawrence Erlbaum, 1994), p. 331.

4   "Sunbeams," *Sun Magazine*, January 2009, p. 48.

5   John Daly taught me to think about communication like this.

CHAPTER 5

1   Penelope Brown and Stephen Levinson, "Politeness: Some Universals in Language Usage," in *Studies in Interactional Sociolinguistics*, ed. John J. Gumperz (Cambridge: Cambridge University Press, 1987), vol. 4, pp. 59–62.

2   Sarah Bakewell, *How to Live: A Life of Montaigne* (New York: Other Press, 2010), p. 109.

3   I posted an early version of this list on my website at http://mouthpeaceconsulting.com on January 23, 2012.

4   John Gottman and Nan Silver, *The Seven Principles for Making Marriage Work* (New York: Three Rivers Press, 1999), pp. 22–23. Gott-

man and Silver use the term *repair attempt* to describe containment during an escalated conversation.

5 The line from the movie, about down-on-their-luck salesmen, is *always be closing*.

CHAPTER 6

1 Confucius, *Confucian Analects, the Great Learning, and the Doctrine of the Mean*, trans. James Legge (New York: Dover, 1971), p. 250.

2 My thinking about how easy it is to spot dumb statements in the digital age, but how hard it is to erase them, was spurred by Schumpeter, "When Stars Go Cuckoo," *Economist*, March 3, 2011, http://www.economist.com/node/18277161.

3 John Suler, "The Online Disinhibition Effect," *Cyber-Psychology and Behavior*, vol. 7, no. 3 (2004), pp. 321–322, doi:10.1089/1094931041291295.

4 Thanks to Mark Knapp for pointing out the redirection strategy.

CHAPTER 7

1 Gaston de Lévis, *Maximes et Réflections sur Différents Sujets de Morale et de Politique* (Paris, 1810), under Maxim XVII, available online through Google books.

2 See Steven A. Holmes, "James Stockdale, Perot's Running Mate in '92, Dies at 81," *New York Times*, July 6, 2005, http://www.nytimes.com /2005/07/06/politics/06stockdale.html. See also "Vice-Admiral James Stockdale," *The Telegraph*, July 7, 2005, http://www.telegraph.co.uk/news/obituaries/1493505/Vice-Admiral-James-Stockdale.html.

3 Charles J. Stewart and William B. Cash, *Interviewing: Principles and Practices*, 10th ed. (New York: McGraw-Hill, 2003), pp. 56–57.

4 Note that statements like "Please tell me more about your idea" and "Please describe the Gatorville account proposal" are technically punctuated with periods, but in practice they function as queries.

5 Stewart and Cash, *Interviewing*, pp. 57–59.

6 Ibid., p. 61. What Stewart and Cash call *nudging probes* I simplify to *nudges*. Also note that the terms *leading questions* and *loaded questions* from earlier in the chapter are commonly used by researchers (including Stewart and Cash, pp. 65–68) and others in question classification schemes.

CHAPTER 8

1   I use the terms *strategic conversation* and *important conversation* interchangeably, since a strategic conversation is an important one and vice versa.

2   An early version of GAS appeared on my blog at http://mouthpeaceconsulting.com on April 2, 2012.

3   Daniel Kahneman, *Thinking, Fast and Slow* (New York: Farrar, Straus and Giroux, 2011), pp. 380–381.

CHAPTER 9

1   "Internet 2012 in Numbers," *Royal Pingdom* (blog), January 16, 2013, http://royal.pingdom.com/2013/01/16/internet-2012-in-numbers/, and "Internet 2011 in Numbers," *Royal Pingdom* (blog), January 17, 2012, http://royal.pingdom.com/2012/01/17/internet-2011-in-numbers/. See also "Key Statistical Highlights: ITU Data release June 2012," ITU World Telecommunications/ICT Indicators Database, June 2012, http://www.itu.int/ITU-D/ict/statistics/material/pdf/2011%20Statistical%20highlights_June_2012. pdf, and "Internet 2010 in Numbers," *Royal Pingdom* (blog), January 12, 2011, http://royal.pingdom.com/2011/01/12/internet-2010-in-numbers/.

2   Dominique Jean Larrey, *Memoir of Baron Larrey: Surgeon-in-Chief of the Grande Army* (London: Henry Renshaw, 1861; facsimile edition produced by Kessinger Publishing, 2010). See also Jose M. Ortiz, "The Revolutionary Flying Ambulance of Napoleon's Surgeon," *U.S. Army Medical Department Journal*, October–December 1998, pp. 17–25, http://cdm16379.contentdm.oclc.org/cdm/ref/collection/p15290coll3/id/527.

3   Sheri Fink, "The Deadly Choices at Memorial," *New York Times Magazine*, August 25, 2009, http://www.nytimes.com/2009/08/30/magazine/30doctors.html.

4   You should be the one to determine if you are dealing with a time-sensitive problem. The person presenting the issue is predisposed to think that it's a time-sensitive issue.

5   If any of these people bring you problems constantly, see the *Trouble with the A Team* section from Chapter 3 for suggestions.

6   Incidentally, Larrey's triage system worked so well for the Grand Armée that Napoleon bequeathed Larrey 100,000 francs in his last will and testament. Napoleon wrote, "He is the most virtuous man I have ever known" (Larrey, *Memoir*, p. 256).

CHAPTER 10

1   Lee Ross and Craig A. Anderson, "Shortcomings in the Attribution Process: On the Origins and Maintenance of Erroneous Social Assessments," in *Judgment Under Uncertainty: Heuristics and Biases*, ed. Daniel Kahneman, Paul Slovic, and Amos Tversky (Cambridge: Cambridge University Press: 1982), pp. 135–138.

2   I'm recommending quick apologies to take advantage of the amnesty period that is often available immediately after an error, especially when the error is relatively small, like a verbal slip or minor transgression that doesn't touch on an identity issue. As the magnitude of the error increases, there's some evidence that people prefer a bit of time to pass so they feel "ready" for the apology; see Cynthia McPherson Frantz and Courtney Bennigson, "Better Late Than Early: The Influence of Timing on Apology Effectiveness," *Journal of Experimental Social Psychology*, vol. 41, no. 2 (2005), pp. 205–206, doi: 10.1016/j.jesp.2004.07.007. Crucially, Frantz and Bennigson's research finds that any apology—early or delayed—is better than no apologies, reinforcing our preferred strategy of apologizing immediately following a transgression. If the other person isn't ready for the apology, you can always apologize again later. For a good general discussion of timeliness in apologies, see Aaron Lazare, *On Apology* (New York: Oxford University Press, 2004), pp. 170–203.

3   Robert B. Cialdini, *Influence: Science and Practice*, 4th ed. (Boston: Allyn and Bacon, 2001), pp. 52–55.

4   Steven J. Scher and John M. Darley, "How Effective Are the Things People Say to Apologize? Effects of the Realization of the Apology Speech Act," *Journal of Psycholinguistic Research*, vol. 26, no. 1 (1997), p. 132, doi: 10.1023/A:1025068306386.

5   Ibid., p. 136.

6   Jane McGonigal, *Reality Is Broken: Why Games Make Us Better and How They Can Change the World* (New York: Penguin, 2011), pp. 207–208.

CHAPTER 11

1   Josh Peter, *Fried Twinkies, Buckle Bunnies, and Bull Riders: A Year Inside the Professional Bull Riders Tour* (Emmaus, PA: Rodale, 2005), pp. 78–79.

2   "Tuff Hedeman & Bodacious Clip - A Promise to a Son," YouTube video, 4:35, posted by rwillie22, July 10, 2011, http://www.youtube.com/watch?v=mRKb0Q5Nj9s, and "Tuff Guy: Bull Rider Hedeman Endures Injury, Grief to Stay on Top," *CNN Sports Illustrated*,

October 7, 1997, http://sportsillustrated.cnn.com/more/rodeo/
news/1997/10/07/tuff_hedeman.

3   "Tuff Hedeman & Bodacious Clip - A Promise to a Son," YouTube
    video, 4:35, posted by rwillie22, July 10, 2011, http://www.youtube.
    com/watch?v=mRKb0Q5Nj9s.

4   "Staff," Championship Bull Riding (CBR) biography of Tuff
    Hedeman, accessed April 21, 2013, http://www.cbrbull.com/staff.
    html?people_id=13.

5   Roland Lazenby, *Mindgames: Phil Jackson's Long Strange Journey* (Chi-
    cago: Contemporary Books, 2001), pp. 207–210.

6   Dennis Rodman, *Bad as I Wanna Be*, with Tim Keown (New York:
    Delacorte, 1996), pp. 253–254.

7   See Phil Jackson and Hugh Delehanty, *Sacred Hoops: Spiritual Lessons
    of a Hardwood Warrior* (New York: Hyperion, 2006), pp. 43–58 and
    97–112.

8   Ibid., p. 168.

9   We discuss two other common types of difficult people, verbally
    aggressive (bullies) and excitement addicts, in Chapters 12 and 15,
    respectively.

CHAPTER 12

1   Harry Haymaker is *definitely* a pseudonym. I still see Harry at my
    college reunions, and in light of his boxing technique, I don't want
    to upset him.

2   It turns out that the ability to pretend I was fighting would serve
    me well during my service in the peacetime army. I would use
    the skill again during Ranger School, where I augmented my fake
    fighting skills with bloodcurdling screams in a spectacle that would
    make a professional wrestler blush. When I arrived at my first army
    unit in Hawaii, I assumed that fake fighting was comfortably behind
    me. Imagine my surprise (and dismay) when I learned that my unit
    was going to implement a combatives program—combatives being
    a euphemism for punching and kicking each other during morning
    physical training. For a third and mercifully final time, I dusted off
    my skills, screamed like my hair was on fire, and pulled my punches
    (as did everyone else) during the combatives training. As I have
    repeatedly told my wife, if we ever get mugged I might not *actually*
    be able to save us, but it will surely *sound* like I am saving us.

3   Daniel Goleman, *Social Intelligence: The New Science of Human Rela-
    tionships* (New York: Bantam Dell, 2007), pp. 230–232.

4   Two books provide excellent overviews and practical advice based on Gottman and colleagues' research: John M. Gottman and Nan Silver, *The Seven Principles for Making Marriage Work* (New York: Three Rivers Press, 1999), and John M. Gottman, Julie Schwartz Gottman, and Joan DeClaire, *Ten Lessons to Transform Your Marriage* (New York: Three Rivers Press, 2006). The claim about predicting marital success or dissolution with 90 percent accuracy is found on page 2 of *The Seven Principles* and page 1 of *Ten Lessons*. Gottman's research methodology is explained in detail in John Mordechai Gottman, *What Predicts Divorce? The Relationship Between Marital Processes and Marital Outcomes* (Hillsdale, NJ: Lawrence Erlbaum, 1994).

5   I posted an early version of this list on my blog at http://mouth-peaceconsulting.com on May 28, 2012.

6   Mark L. Knapp and Anita L. Vangelisti, *Interpersonal Communication and Human Relationships*, 4th ed. (Boston: Allyn and Bacon, 2000), pp. 12–13. See also Barbara L. Fredrickson, *Love 2.0: How Our Supreme Emotion Affects Everything We Feel, Think, Do, and Become* (New York: Hudson Street, 2013), pp. 21–27 and Goleman, *Social Intelligence*, pp. 30–35.

7   Mark L. Knapp, John A. Daly, and Laura Stafford, "Regrettable Messages: Things People Wish They Hadn't Said," *Journal of Communication*, vol. 36, no. 4 (1986), pp. 48–49.

8   Paulo Coelho, *The Alchemist*, trans. Alan R. Clarke (New York: HarperSanFrancisco, 1998), p. 156.

9   In your personal life, you might decide to grant blanket verbal clemency to elderly family members. As a general communication principle, as people get closer to the end of their life, it's smart to be increasingly forgiving of anything they may say.

CHAPTER 13

1   James O. Prochaska, Carlo C. DiClemente, and John C. Norcross, "In Search of How People Change: Applications to Addictive Behaviors," *American Psychologist*, vol. 47, no. 9 (September 1992), pp. 1102–1105, doi: 10.1037/0003-066X.47.9.1102. For Prochaska and colleagues' practical guide to behavioral change, see James O. Prochaska, John C. Norcross, and Carlo C. DiClemente, *Changing for Good: A Revolutionary Six-Stage Program for Overcoming Bad Habits and Moving Your Life Positively Forward* (New York: Avon Books, 1994).

2   Philip Zimbardo, "Pathology of Imprisonment," *Society*, vol. 9, no. 6 (1972), pp. 4–6, doi: 10.1007/BF02701755.

3   The bad apple–rotten barrel analogy is widely used by teachers discussing ethics; for example, see Linda K. Trevino and Katherine A. Nelson, *Managing Business Ethics: Straight Talk About How to Do It Right*, 5th ed. (Hoboken, NJ: John Wiley & Sons, 2011), p. 19.

4   John M. Darley and C. Daniel Batson, " 'From Jerusalem to Jericho': A Study of Situational and Dispositional Variables in Helping Behavior," *Journal of Personality and Social Psychology*, vol. 27, no. 1 (1973), pp. 104–105, doi: 10.1037/h0034449. Note that it was being in a hurry that influenced (reduced) helping behavior, not the topic of the speech.

5   Howard Giles and Nikolas Coupland, *Language: Contexts and Consequences* (Pacific Grove, CA: Brooks/Cole, 1991), pp. 60–74.

6   For a review of research on the impact of situational factors on leader and follower behaviors, see Bernard M. Bass, "Environment and Organizational Effects," chap. 25 in *The Bass Handbook of Leadership*, with Ruth Bass (New York: Free Press, 2008), pp. 716–755. For a general discussion of situational influences on ethical organizational behavior, see Trevino and Nelson, *Managing Business Ethics*, pp. 18–19. For a discussion of how situational factors influence prosocial behaviors, see Trevino and Nelson, *Managing Business Ethics*, pp. 292–294.

7   Daniel Goleman, *Social Intelligence: The New Science of Human Relationships* (New York: Bantam Dell, 2007), pp. 31–35. See also Robert B. Cialdini, *Influence: Science and Practice*, 4th ed. (Boston: Allyn and Bacon, 2001), pp. 100–111, and Giles and Coupland, *Language*, pp. 62–71.

8   If you find yourself on the receiving end of feedback, remember the *rule of 10*. People can avoid uncomfortable issues for a long time, so if someone is instigating a direct conversation with you to deliver negative feedback, assume your behavior is impacting more than one person and multiply the negative feedback by 10. If someone tells you that your pointed questions upset him, assume that at least 10 other people don't like your questioning technique either. If a client says that you aren't being responsive to her needs, infer that 10 other clients are probably having the same issue.

9   Focusing on the problem and not the person is a classic tenet of effective negotiation popularized by Roger Fisher and William Ury, *Getting to Yes,* ed. Bruce Patton (New York: Penguin Books, 1983), pp. 17–40.

CHAPTER 14

1 Mark Twain, *Following the Equator* (Hartford, CT: American Publishing, 1898; Project Gutenberg, 1996), part 3, chap. 20 epigraph, http://www.gutenberg.org/files/2895/old/orig2895-h/p3.htm.

2 Daphna Oysterman, "Self-Concept and Identity," in *Self and Social Identity*, ed. Marilynn B. Brewer and Miles Hewstone (Malden, MA: Blackwell, 2004), p. 9.

3 Miller McPherson, Lynn Smith-Lovin, and James M. Cook, "Birds of a Feather: Homophily in Social Networks," *Annual Review of Sociology*, vol. 27 (2001), pp. 415–429, esp. p. 429, doi: 10.1146/annurev. soc.27.1.415.

4 Carl W. Backman and Paul F. Secord, "Liking, Selective Interaction, and Misperception in Congruent Interpersonal Relations," *Sociometry*, vol. 25, no. 4 (1962), p. 335, doi: 10.2307/2785772.

5 S. Alexander Haslam, *Psychology in Organizations: The Social Identity Approach* (London: Sage, 2001), p. 53.

6 For a review of group polarization research, see Bill Bishop, *The Big Sort: Why the Clustering of Like-Minded America Is Tearing Us Apart, with Robert G. Cushing* (New York: Houghton Mifflin, 2008), pp. 63–70.

7 Don Richardson, ed., *Conversations with Carter* (Boulder, CO: Lynne Rienner, 1998), pp. 56–57.

8 Ibid., p. 58.

9 Jimmy Carter, *Living Faith* (New York: Times Books, 1996), pp. 127–129.

10 Richardson, *Conversations with Carter*, p. 2.

11 For a good overview of identity and self-presentation, see Sam Gosling, *Snoop: What Your Stuff Says About You* (New York: Basic Books, 2008), pp. 66–112, esp. pp. 66–85.

12 I posted a version of SLOW on my blog at http://mouthpeaceconsulting.com on October 22, 2012.

CHAPTER 15

1 Roy F. Baumeister and John Tierney, *Willpower: Rediscovering the Greatest Human Strength* (New York: Penguin, 2011), p. 245.

2 Karen S. Rook, "Investigating the Positive and Negative Sides of Personal Relationships: Through a Lens Darkly?," in *The Dark Side of Close Relationships*, ed. Brian H. Spitzberg and William R. Cupach (Mahwah, NJ: Lawrence Erlbaum, 1998), pp. 376–377.

CHAPTER 16

1   "Key Facts," Facebook Newsroom, accessed November 7, 2012, http://newsroom.fb.com/Key-Facts; and "Statistics," YouTube Press Room, accessed November 7, 2012, http://www.youtube.com/t/press_statistics.

2   John A. Daly and Anita L. Vangelisti, "Skillfully Instructing Learners: How Communicators Effectively Convey Messages," in *Handbook of Communication and Social Interaction Skills*, ed. John O. Greene and Brant R. Burleson (Mahwah, NJ: Lawrence Erlbaum, 2003), pp. 881–882. For a general discussion of stories in business, see Daniel H. Pink, *A Whole New Mind: Why Right-Brainers Will Rule the Future* (New York: Riverhead Books, 2006), pp. 100–115.

3   Daly and Vangelisti, "Skillfully Instructing Learners," pp. 881–882.

4   There is a fine line between simplification and oversimplification. The goal of simplification, as Albert Einstein said when talking about theory, is to "make the irreducible basic elements as simple and as few as possible without having to surrender the adequate representation of a single datum of experience." "On the Method of Theoretical Physics," *Philosophy of Science*, vol. 1, no. 2 (April 1934), p. 165, doi: 10.1086/286316.

5   John A. Daly, *Advocacy: Championing Ideas and Influencing Others* (New Haven, CT: Yale University Press, 2011), pp. 264–268.

6   Nassim Nicholas Taleb, *The Black Swan: The Impact of the Highly Improbable* (New York: Random House, 2007), pp. 63–64. See also Daniel Kahneman, *Thinking, Fast and Slow* (New York: Farrar, Straus and Giroux, 2011), pp. 199–202.

7   See James Geary, *I Is an Other* (New York: Harper, 2011), pp. 5–16. See also Daly, *Advocacy*, pp. 280–286, and James Geary, *The World in a Phrase* (New York: Bloomsbury, 2005), pp. 8–20.

8   This story by Ron Evans, referred to as "The Storyteller," was recorded at the 1982 National Storytelling Festival in Jonesboro, Tennessee, and later released on an audiocassette produced by the National Association for the Preservation and Perpetuation of Storytelling. Thanks to Peninnah Schram for bringing this story to my attention.

RECOMMENDED READING

In addition to sources listed in the notes, the following books are recommended for additional reading on topics discussed in *Stop Talking, Start Communicating*.

Axelrod, Robert. *The Evolution of Cooperation.* New York: Basic Books, 1984.

Baron, Naomi B. *Always On: Language in an Online World.* New York: Oxford University Press, 2008.

Beach, Lee Roy. *Leadership and the Art of Change: A Practical Guide to Organizational Transformation.* Thousand Oaks, CA: Sage, 2006.

Buonomano, Dean. *Brain Bugs: How the Brain's Flaws Shape Our Lives.* New York: W. W. Norton, 2011.

Cain, Susan. *Quiet: The Power of Introverts in a World That Can't Stop Talking.* New York: Crown, 2012.

Christian, Brian. *The Most Human Human: What Talking with Computers Teaches Us About What It Means to Be Alive.* New York: Doubleday, 2011.

Coleman, Peter T. *The Five Percent: Finding Solutions to Seemingly Impossible Conflicts.* With contributions from the faculty of the International Project on Conflict and Complexity. New York: PublicAffairs, 2011.

de Graff, John, David Wann, and Thomas H. Naylor. *Affluenza: The All-Consuming Epidemic,* 2nd ed. In association with Redefining Progress; with new research by Pamela Rands. San Francisco: Berrett-Koehler, 2005.

de Zengotita, Thomas. *Mediated: How the Media Shapes Your World and the Way You Live in It.* New York: Bloomsbury, 2005.

Duhigg, Charles. *The Power of Habit: Why We Do What We Do in Life and Business.* New York: Random House, 2012.

Frijda, Nico H. *The Laws of Emotion.* Mahwah, NJ: Lawrence Erlbaum, 2007.

Gardner, John W. *Living, Leading, and the American Dream.* Edited by Francesca Gardner. San Francisco: Jossey-Bass, 2003.

Giddens, Anthony. *Runaway World: How Globalization Is Reshaping Our Lives*. London: Profile Books, 1999.

Goffman, Erving. *Interaction Ritual: Essays on Face-to-Face Behavior*. New York: Pantheon Books, 1982.

Goffman, Erving. *The Presentation of Self in Everyday Life*. New York: Anchor Books, 1959.

Goldsmith, Marshall. *What Got You Here Won't Get You There: How Successful People Become Even More Successful!* With Mark Reiter. New York: Hyperion, 2007.

Gottschall, Jonathan. *The Storytelling Animal: How Stories Make Us Human*. Boston: Houghton Mifflin Harcourt, 2012.

Gratton, Lynda. *The Shift: The Future of Work Is Already Here*. London: Collins, 2011.

Harper, Richard H. R. *Texture: Human Expression in the Age of Communications Overload*. Cambridge, MA: MIT Press, 2010.

Heath, Chip, and Dan Heath. *Switch: How to Change Things When Change Is Hard*. New York: Broadway Books, 2010.

Kay, John. *Obliquity: Why Our Goals Are Best Achieved Indirectly*. New York: Penguin Press, 2011.

Keizer, Garret. *Privacy*. New York: Picador, 2012.

Klingberg, Torkel. *The Overflowing Brain: Information Overload and the Limits of Working Memory*. New York: Oxford University Press, 2009.

Koch, Richard. *The 80/20 Principle: The Secret to Success by Achieving More with Less*. New York: Currency Doubleday, 1998.

LeDoux, Joseph. *The Emotional Brain: The Mysterious Underpinnings of Emotional Life*. New York: Simon & Schuster Paperbacks, 1996.

Levmore, Saul, and Martha C. Nussbaum, eds. *The Offensive Internet: Privacy, Speech, and Reputation*. Cambridge, MA: Harvard University Press, 2010.

Maushart, Susan. *The Winter of Our Disconnect: How Three Totally Wired Teenagers (and a Mother Who Slept with Her iPhone) Pulled the Plug on Their Technology and Lived to Tell the Tale*. New York: Jeremy P. Tarcher/Penguin, 2010.

McAdams, Dan P. *The Stories We Live By: Personal Myths and the Making of the Self*. New York: William Morrow, 1993.

Meadows, Donella H. *Thinking in Systems: A Primer*. Edited by Diana Wright. White River Junction, VT: Chelsea Green, 2008.

Morozov, Evgeny. *The Net Delusion: The Dark Side of Internet Freedom.* New York: PublicAffairs, 2011.

Nass, Clifford. *The Man Who Lied to His Laptop: What Machines Teach Us About Human Relationships.* With Corina Yen. New York: Current, 2010.

Nerburn, Kent. *Simple Truths: Clear and Gentle Guidance on the Big Issues in Life.* Novato, CA: New World Library, 1996.

Pariser, Eli. *The Filter Bubble: What the Internet Is Hiding from You.* New York: Penguin Press, 2011.

Partnoy, Frank. *Wait: The Art and Science of Delay.* New York: PublicAffairs, 2012.

Patterson, Kerry, Joseph Grenny, Ron McMillan, and Al Switzler. *Crucial Conversations: Tools for Talking When Stakes Are High,* 2nd ed. New York: McGraw-Hill, 2012.

Pfeffer, Jeffrey. *Power: Why Some People Have It—and Others Don't.* New York: Harper Business, 2010.

Pfeffer, Jeffrey, and Robert I. Sutton. *The Knowing-Doing Gap: How Smart Companies Turn Knowledge into Action.* Boston: Harvard Business School Press, 2000.

Pink, Daniel H. *Drive: The Surprising Truth About What Motivates Us.* New York: Riverhead Books, 2009.

Potter, Andrew. *The Authenticity Hoax: How We Get Lost Finding Ourselves.* New York: Harper, 2010.

Powers, William. *Hamlet's Blackberry: A Practical Philosophy for Building a Good Life in the Digital Age.* New York: Harper, 2010.

Prochnik, George. *In Pursuit of Silence: Listening for Meaning in a World of Noise.* New York: Doubleday, 2010.

Rao, Srikumar S. *Are You Ready to Succeed? Unconventional Strategies for Achieving Personal Mastery in Business and Life.* New York: Hyperion, 2006.

Rosenzweig, Phil. *The Halo Effect . . . and the Eight Other Business Delusions That Deceive Managers.* New York: Free Press, 2009.

Schulz, Kathryn. *Being Wrong: Adventures in the Margin of Error.* New York: Ecco, 2010.

Scott, Susan. *Fierce Conversations: Achieving Success at Work and in Life, One Conversation at a Time.* New York: Viking, 2002.

Seidman, Dov. *How: Why How We Do Anything Means Everything . . . in Business (and in Life).* Hoboken, NJ: John Wiley & Sons, 2007.

Solove, Daniel J. *The Future of Reputation: Gossip, Rumor, and Privacy on the Internet.* New Haven, CT: Yale University Press, 2007.

Sternberg, Robert J. *Why Smart People Can Be So Stupid.* New Haven, CT: Yale University Press, 2002.

Taleb, Nassim Nicholas. *Antifragile: Things That Gain from Disorder.* New York: Random House, 2012.

Taleb, Nassim Nicholas. *Fooled by Randomness: The Hidden Role of Chance in Life and in the Markets,* 2nd ed. New York: Random House Trade Paperbacks, 2005.

Turkle, Sherry. *The Second Self: Computers and the Human Spirit.* New York: Simon & Schuster, 1984.

Whybrow, Peter C. *American Mania: When More Is Not Enough.* New York: W. W. Norton, 2006.

Wilson, Timothy D. *Redirect: The Surprising New Science of Psychological Change.* New York: Little, Brown, 2011.

ACKNOWLEDGMENTS

Now I know why authors thank so many people in this section.

My parents, Ron and Daphne Tumlin, read every word of numerous drafts and provided tireless editorial support. I'm grateful for their assistance. Jane Ryder introduced me to the brilliant Beth Jusino, who provided indispensable manuscript advice and thorough editing.

Morgan Roth and Ulla Schnell connected me to Jessica Papin, my invaluable, thoughtful, and resourceful agent, who came up with the book's title and so much more. My instant and authentic connection with Casey Ebro, my editor at McGraw-Hill, translated into a delightful working relationship. Janice Race and Judy Duguid made the production process smooth and enjoyable. I sincerely appreciate Janice's patience and professionalism. Thanks to Jason Santamaria for putting in the good word with Mary Glenn at McGraw-Hill.

Justin Pritchard and Jeremy Stout helped me clarify my initial thoughts about the book. Wanda Granberry graciously shared her time and expertise to help me improve an early version of the manuscript. Karen Tumlin, Betty Chapman, and Karon Bowers also provided early and important input.

Mark Knapp and John Daly indelibly shaped my thinking about communication, and Howard Prince did the same for leadership. I wouldn't have systematically studied communication without Mark; I wouldn't have developed as a teacher without John; and I wouldn't have acquired an integrated understanding of leadership without Howard. I'm grateful that they shared their knowledge with me. At the University of Texas at Austin, the Department of

Communication Studies and the LBJ School of Public Affairs were fruitful homes for a decade.

In business, Rebecca Henley is my right-hand woman. I couldn't do a fraction of the things I do without her. Thanks to our clients who provided many of the experiences that shaped this book. Thanks to Martha Mendoza for contributing the Foreword, and thanks to all the endorsers. My gratitude goes to Peninnah Schram for graciously granting permission to use her story, "The Power of the Tongue."

Margaret Keys, Steven Tomlinson, and Nancy Graves helped me become a better observer of people. Lally Brennan, Ti Martin, Tory McPhail, Jimmy Boudreaux, Joe Pilie, Jenny Giannobile, and Billy Langston welcomed me like family during writing breaks at Commander's Palace that were all too infrequent. Icy and Miles Donnelly and Stephen Warner did the same at La Frite. Gregory Thomas-Tench helped me get my ideas online, answered dozens of questions cheerfully, and somehow had the equanimity to laugh when I crashed his servers.

Others who provided assistance in various ways include: Tina Morris, Paul Martorana, Jen and Jim Betancourt, Tom Pace, Bernie Skown, Joe Youngblood, Mike Moonbeam Weathers, Nick Lennon, Rob Morris, Pete Von Alt, Anita Vangelisti, Madeline Maxwell, Roger Tumlin, Calvin Belbin, Amy Schmisseur, Stacey Connaughton, Brian Richardson, Ethan Burris, Hector Diaz, Maru Gonzalez, Iris and Felix Pritchard, Peter Frumkin, Nancy Sims, the Battistoni family, Annella Metoyer, Lynn Luppino, David Moldawer, Daniel Ambrosio, Betty Wilkes, Evelyn Schilling, Scott Kopetz, Eleanor Belbin, Bobbie Smith, Sandy Eckhardt, David Pearson, Quang Ngo, Dawn Haberkorn, and Tim Taliaferro.

Thanks and much more to Cindi Baldi, wife and friend.

INDEX

ABOUT THE AUTHOR

Geoffrey Tumlin is the founder and CEO of Mouthpeace Consulting LLC, a communication consulting company; president of On-Demand Leadership, a leadership development company; and founder and board chair of Critical Skills Nonprofit, a 501(c)(3) public charity dedicated to providing communication and leadership skills training to chronically underserved populations. His writing on communication and leadership has appeared in scholarly journals, newspapers, and textbooks, including *Discourse Studies*, the *International Leadership Journal*, the *Encyclopedia of Leadership*, the *Austin American-Statesman*, and five editions of *Professional Communication Skills*.

Tumlin holds a PhD and an MA in communication from the University of Texas at Austin and a BS from West Point. He received the Eyes of Texas Excellence Award in 2010 for his work as the assistant director of the Center for Ethical Leadership at the University of Texas at Austin. He was a Faculty Fellow at the University of Texas at Austin's RGK Center for Philanthropy and Community Service and a Cátedras Laboris Fellow at the University of Monterrey in Nuevo León, Mexico.

Tumlin currently serves as trustee of the National Communication Association's Mark L. Knapp Award Individual Endowment, the most prestigious interpersonal communication honor bestowed annually by the National Communication Association in recognition of career contributions to the academic study of interpersonal communication. Tumlin has taught thousands of people about communication and leadership and has consulted with some of the most prestigious organizations in the world, including Shell Oil, Wyeth Pharmaceuticals, the Boston Scientific Corporation, Hibernia National Bank (now Capital One Bank), Blue Star Management, and the Honolulu Police Department. He lives in Austin, Texas.

You can learn more about Geoff Tumlin at www.tumlin.com, and you can reach him by e-mail at geoff@tumlin.com.